little *pink* book
A Survival Guide for Women

Copyright ©2019 by Hope Carpenter Ministries

All Rights Reserved. This book is protected under the copyright laws of the United States of America. This book and any portion thereof may not be copied or reprinted for commercial gain or profit. The use of short quotations or occasional page copying for personal or group study is permitted and encouraged.

ISBN 978-0-578-44767-4

Printed in the United States of America

Published by
Hope Carpenter Ministries
105 Nortech Parkway
San Jose, California 95134
www.hopecarpenter.com

contents

- A Note from Pastor Hope 7
- Devotional Guides 9
- What to Do When 15
- Recipes 47
  - Appetizers 48
  - Side Dishes 57
  - Main Dishes 70
  - Desserts 83
  - Cooking Measurements 98
- Table Manners 101
- Beauty Tips 109
  - International Clothes & Shoe Size Chart 120
- Body Talk 122
- Health/Fitness 125
- DYI Projects 133
- Organizational Hacks 143
- Date Night Ideas 151

> Breakthrough comes when you decide to break free.
> *Pastor Hope Carpenter*

She searches out continually to possess that which is pure and righteous.
She delights in the work of her hands She gives
out revelation-truth to feed others.
She is like a trading ship bringing divine supplies from the merchant.
Even in the night season she arises and sets food on
the table for hungry ones in her house and for others.
She sets her heart upon a nation and takes it as
her own, carrying it within her.
She labors there to plant the living vines.
She wraps herself in strength, might, and power in all her works.
She tastes and experiences a better substance, and her shining light
will not be extinguished, no matter how dark the night.
She stretches out her hands to help the needy
and she lays hold of the wheels of government.
She is known by her extravagant generosity to the poor,
for she always reaches out her hands to those in need.
She is not afraid of tribulation, for all her household is covered
in the dual garments of righteousness and grace.
Her clothing is beautifully knit together a purple gown of exquisite linen.
Proverbs 31:13-22

> A giant in front of you
> is never bigger
> than the God
> inside of you.
> *Pastor Hope Carpenter*

a note from pastor hope...

For all of you beautiful ladies out there: daughters, sisters, mothers, wives, CEOs, school teachers, stay at home moms, nurses, bloggers, and all of the 1,000 other titles we wear. Do not think for one minute that you are less than any other woman out there! You are exactly who you were created to be. Does that mean that there isn't room for improvement? That you can't become the best version of You? Absolutely not. Become a lifelong learner. Read daily. Stay humble. Be quick to forgive and take the advice of a little rabbit, "if you can't say nothing nice, don't say anything at all".

I pray that this Little Pink Book helps you survive in this journey called life!

Cheerfully,

Hope Carpenter

> If we're fighting each other we can't fight the enemy.
>
> *Pastor Hope Carpenter*

devotional guides

> "
>
> Your devotions may have seemed ordinary today, but God is making something extraordinary through it.
>
> "
>
> DesiringGod.org

· Devotional Guides ·

Praise … When I witness praise, submission and the moving of the Holy Spirit during a worship service, my heart is overwhelmed within me to think of the stories behind each individual's praise. Praise His name forever. *Psalms 145:1 [TPT] My heart explodes with praise to you! Now and forever my heart bows in worship to you, my King and my God!*

∼ *Kimberly Woody* ∼

Faith … Faith (mental movement toward God) with the Holy Spirit fruits (love, joy, peace, long suffering, kindness, goodness, faithfulness, gentleness, self-control) develops righteousness. *Galatians 5:1 Stand Fast … ; 2 Corinthians 1:24 … for by faith ye stand.*

Faith is believing that God can help you out of every bondage you might be in. He will help you out of every bondage you are in. Let God help you starting now.

Brokenness and Despair is only for a short time. Look up your redeemer is near. *Isaiah 60:1-4, … Lift up thine eyes round about, and see; Isaiah 59:20-21, … And the Redeemer shall come to Zion, and unto them that turn from transgression in Jacob, saith the LORD.* Remember keep your head up and keep faith in God — *Philippians 4:13 I can do all things through Christ which strengthen me.*

P-I-N-K » P-Psalms | I-Isaiah | N-Nehemiah | K-Kings
Old Testament books that will inspire and strengthen you.

Pray the holy scriptures concerning your situation while believing it is already completed. Do this every day and be patient with the manifestations.

∼ *Florence Jones* ∼

· Devotional Guides ·

Personal Reflection … Write a letter to your thirteen-year-old self. This is fun, thought provoking, and a reflective moment to think about yourself when you were a young teenager. What are those things you will caution yourself on? Is there a bible verse or life experience you use now that could've helped you then? What will you tell yourself to look forward to? Are you doing what you set out in life to do? What would you change? Lastly, how has your faith made you who you are today? If you have young kids or grandkids, share your letter with them. And if you have a child, have them write the same type of letter but to their 21 year-old self. I did this with my son and it was a wonderful experience.

≈ *Vecepia Robinson* ≈

Marriage … No matter how angry my husband and I are with each other we never leave home or come home without giving each other a kiss and saying "I love you." Just because we are angry does not mean we stop loving each other. It prevents the awkwardness and doesn't allow the enemy to cause more strife between us.

≈ *Belinda Coleman* ≈

A really great devotional guide for women is the "Princess" series of books created by Sherri Rose. There are 3 different titles you can purchase "His Princess", "Princess Bride" and "Princess Warrior". Each one of the books is a love letter from your king and based upon scripture.

≈ *Chinere McDaniels* ≈

• Devotional Guides •

When worry is getting the best of you ... *Fight in Faith*. I've been encouraged by this book, "Winning the Worry Battle" by Barb Roose. Inspired by the book of Joshua, the writer reviews three tools a person can develop to *Fight In Faith*: 1) Embracing God's promises, 2) Courage and commitment under pressure and 3) Practicing radical obedience while waiting for God to deliver your victory.

~ *Denise Howe* ~

Have you ever acted on your feelings?? Reacted? Responded? Spoken out? Gave someone a piece of your mind? Yup, me too, unfortunately! Our feelings are not always truth!!! Feelings change by situations and even our chemicals in the brain! Don't be fooled by the Devil! We got to learn to rise above our feelings and only respond, and speak the truth of God's word! What does GOD SAY about whatever situation you are in right now???? Say that! Don't be a tool of the enemy today!!! (God's really on me about this one)

Pastor Hope Carpenter

· Devotional Guides ·

Love … "And just because a person left you or hurt you doesn't mean he or she is a buffoon. Nor does it mean they are a bad person. But rather they just don't fit in your life anymore. They're no longer a part of the plan God has for you. They were there in your life for a season, but God has someone better and greater in store for you for a lifetime. Walk in it, beloved. Quit holding on to people who don't want to hold on to you. Quit embracing those who are so quick to disregard and throw you away. Does God do that to you? No. His love is never changing. He will never leave you nor forsake you. Hold onto that. Trust in that. Trust in Him. Then let Him lead and guide you to the right people in the right places, those you can truly trust and will love you like God loves you." This is a post that I created and shared through my ministry "Beautiful Truth" Facebook. I published my first book, "180 Days of Beautiful Truth", a daily devotional, last November and it has many nuggets like this, all supported by scripture. You can checkout the book through my website yourbeautifultruth.com.

~ *Sparkle Sanders* ~

Anxiety: When life seems to be moving at a fast pace and everything around me is going crazy, I find it hard to get my spirit still and at peace. I will allow my surroundings to overwhelm me and I will find that anxiousness take over and suddenly I feel defeated. When I start feeling this way, I know its time to get into the Presence of God! The best way to usher in the presence of God is through Worship. He inhabits the praises of His people and if you worship with a pure heart, He will in return give you peace and joy! *Colossians 3:15 Let the peace of Christ rule in your hearts, since as members of one body you were called to peace. And be thankful.*

~ *Chanlin Carpenter Guthrie* ~

> "You can't pull down a stronghold that you support with your lifestyle.
> *Pastor Hope Carpenter*"

what to do when...

> **"**
>
> The devil wants you to pay attention to your feelings. Jesus wants you to pay attention to His truth.
>
> **"**
>
> Hope Carpenter

· What to do when... ·
...you feel *discouraged*

Isaiah 51:11

So the ransomed of the Lord shall return, And come to Zion with singing, with everlasting joy on their heads. They shall obtain joy and gladness; Sorrow and sighing shall flee away.

1 Peter 1:6-9

In this you greatly rejoice, though now for a little while, if need be, you have been grieved by various trials, that the genuineness of your faith, being much more precious than gold that perishes, though it is tested by fire, may be found to praise, honor, and glory at the revelation of Jesus Christ, whom having not seen you love. Though now you do not see Him, yet believing, you rejoice with joy inexpressible and full of glory, receiving the end of your faith—the salvation of your souls.

Philippians 4:6-8

Be anxious for nothing, but in everything by prayer and supplication, with thanksgiving, let your requests be made known to God; and the peace of God, which surpasses all understanding, will guard your hearts and minds through Christ Jesus.

Psalm 31:24

Be of good courage, And He shall strengthen your heart, All you who hope in the Lord.

Psalm 138:7

Though I walk in the midst of trouble, You will revive me; You will stretch out Your hand Against the wrath of my enemies, And Your right hand will save me.

· What to do when … ·

John 14:1
> Let not your heart be troubled; you believe in God, believe also in Me.

John 14:27
> Peace I leave with you, My peace I give to you; not as the world gives do I give to you. Let not your heart be troubled, neither let it be afraid.

2 Corinthians 4:8-9
> You are already full! You are already rich! You have reigned as kings without us—and indeed I could wish you did reign, that we also might reign with you! For I think that God has displayed us, the apostles, last, as men condemned to death; for we have been made a spectacle to the world, both to angels and to men.

Hebrews 10:35-36
> Therefore do not cast away your confidence, which has great reward. 36 For you have need of endurance, so that after you have done the will of God, you may receive the promise.

Phillipians 1:6
> being confident of this very thing, that He who has begun a good work in you will complete it until the day of Jesus Christ.

Galatians 6:9
> And let us not grow weary while doing good, for in due season we shall reap if we do not lose heart.

· What to do when ... ·
...you feel *worried*

1 Peter 5:7
    ...casting all your care upon Him, for He cares for you.

John 14:1
    "Let not your heart be troubled; you believe in God, believe also in Me."

Philippians 4:6-7
    Be anxious for nothing, but in everything by prayer and supplication, with thanksgiving, let your requests be made known to God; and the peace of God, which surpasses all understanding, will guard your hearts and minds through Christ Jesus.

Colossians 3:15
    And let the peace of God rule in your hearts, to which also you were called in one body; and be thankful.

Isaiah 26:3
    You will keep him in perfect peace, Whose mind is stayed on You, Because he trusts in You.

Philippians 4:19
    And my God shall supply all your need according to His riches in glory by Christ Jesus.

Psalm 4:8
    I will both lie down in peace, and sleep; For You alone, O Lord, make me dwell in safety.

· What to do when ... ·

Proverbs 3:24
    When you lie down, you will not be afraid; Yes, you will lie down and your sleep will be sweet.

Psalm 91:1-2
    He who dwells in the secret place of the Most High shall abide under the shadow of the Almighty. I will say of the Lord, "He is my refuge and my fortress;My God, in Him I will trust."

John 14:27
    Peace I leave with you, My peace I give to you; not as the world gives do I give to you. Let not your heart be troubled, neither let it be afraid.

Hebrews 4:3-9
    For we who have believed do enter that rest, as He has said: "So I swore in My wrath, 'They shall not enter My rest,' " although the works were finished from the foundation of the world. For He has spoken in a certain place of the seventh day in this way: "And God rested on the seventh day from all His works"; and again in this place: "They shall not enter My rest." Since therefore it remains that some must enter it, and those to whom it was first preached did not enter because of disobedience, again He designates a certain day, saying in David, "Today," after such a long time, as it has been said: "Today, if you will hear His voice, Do not harden your hearts." For if Joshua had given them rest, then He would not afterward have spoken of another day. There remains therefore a rest for the people of God.

· What to do when ... ·

...you feel *lonely*

Hebrews 13:5
> Let your conduct be without covetousness; be content with such things as you have. For He Himself has said, "I will never leave you nor forsake you."

Matthew 20:29
> Now as they went out of Jericho, a great multitude followed Him.

1 Samuel 12:22
> For the Lord will not forsake His people, for His great name's sake, because it has pleased the Lord to make you His people.

John 14:18
> I will not leave you orphans; I will come to you.

John 14:1
> Let not your heart be troubled; you believe in God, believe also in Me."

Deuteronomy 33:27
> The eternal God is your refuge, and underneath are the everlasting arms;...

Deuteronomy 4:31
> (for the Lord your God is a merciful God), He will not forsake you nor destroy you, nor forget the covenant of your fathers which He swore to them.

Psalm 147:3
> He heals the brokenhearted and binds up their [a]wounds.

· What to do when... ·

Psalm 27:10
When my father and my mother forsake me, then the Lord will take care of me.

1 Peter 5:7
...casting all your care upon Him, for He cares for you.

Psalm 46:1
God is our refuge and strength, a very present help in trouble.

> When you are reduced to nothing,
> God is up to something.
>
> *Pastor Hope Carpenter*

· What to do when ... ·

...you feel *depressed*

Psalm 34:17
>The righteous cry out, and the Lord hears, and delivers them out of all their troubles.

Isaiah 43:2
>When you pass through the waters, I will be with you; And through the rivers, they shall not overflow you. When you walk through the fire, you shall not be burned, Nor shall the flame scorch you.

Psalm 30:5
>For His anger is but for a moment, His favor is for life; Weeping may endure for a night, But joy comes in the morning.

1Peter 4:12-13
>Beloved, do not think it strange concerning the fiery trial which is to try you, as though some strange thing happened to you; 13 but rejoice to the extent that you partake of Christ's sufferings, that when His glory is revealed, you may also be glad with exceeding joy.

Isaiah 61:3
>"To console those who mourn in Zion, to give them beauty for ashes, the oil of joy for mourning, the garment of praise for the spirit of heaviness; That they may be called trees of righteousness, the planting of the Lord, that He may be glorified."

Isaiah 40:31
>But those who wait on the Lord shall renew their strength; They shall mount up with wings like eagles, They shall run and not be weary, they shall walk and not faint.

· What to do when ... ·

Romans 8:38-39
> For I am persuaded that neither death nor life, nor angels nor principalities nor powers, nor things present nor things to come, nor height nor depth, nor any other created thing, shall be able to separate us from the love of God which is in Christ Jesus our Lord.

Philippians 4:8
> Finally, brethren, whatever things are true, whatever things are noble, whatever things are just, whatever things are pure, whatever things are lovely, whatever things are of good report, if there is any virtue and if there is anything praiseworthy—meditate on these things.

Psalm 147:3
> He heals the brokenhearted And binds up theirwounds.

Isaiah 41:10
> Fear not, for I am with you; Be not dismayed, for I am your God. I will strengthen you, Yes, I will help you, I will uphold you with My righteous right hand.'

1 Peter 5:6-7
> Therefore humble yourselves under the mighty hand of God, that He may exalt you in due time, casting all your care upon Him, for He cares for you

Luke 18:1
> Then He spoke a parable to them, that men always ought to pray and not lose heart,...

· What to do when ... ·

Romans 8:1
> There is therefore now no condemnation to those who are in Christ Jesus, who do not walk according to the flesh, but according to the Spirit.

Psalm 103:10 & 12
> He has not dealt with us according to our sins, ... As far as the east is from the west, so far has He removed our transgressions from us. Nor punished us according to our iniquities.

2 Corinthians 5:17
> Therefore, if anyone is in Christ, he is a new creation; old things have passed away; behold, all things have become new.

John 3: 17-18
> "For God did not send His Son into the world to condemn the world, but that the world through Him might be saved. "He who believes in Him is not condemned; but he who does not believe is condemned already, because he has not believed in the name of the only begotten Son of God."

John 5:24
> "Most assuredly, I say to you, he who hears My word and believes in Him who sent Me has everlasting life, and shall not come into judgment, but has passed from death into life."

Isaiah 55:7
> Let the wicked forsake his way, And the unrighteous man his thoughts; Let him return to the Lord, And He will have mercy on him; And to our God, For He will abundantly pardon.

· What to do when ... ·

Hebrews 8:12
"For I will be merciful to their unrighteousness, and their sins and their lawless deeds I will remember no more."

Isaiah 43:25
"I, even I, am He who blots out your transgressions for My own sake; And I will not remember your sins.

Psalm 32:5
I acknowledged my sin to You, And my iniquity I have not hidden. I said, "I will confess my transgressions to the Lord," And You forgave the iniquity of my sin. Selah

1 John 1:9
If we confess our sins, He is faithful and just to forgive us our sins and to cleanse us from all unrighteousness.

Psalm 32:1
Blessed is he whose transgression is forgiven, whose sin is covered.

John 8:10-11
When Jesus had raised Himself up and saw no one but the woman, He said to her, "Woman, where are those accusers of yours? Has no one condemned you?" She said, "No one, Lord." And Jesus said to her, "Neither do I condemn you; go and sin no more."

Hebrews 10:22
...let us draw near with a true heart in full assurance of faith, having our hearts sprinkled from an evil conscience and our bodies washed with pure water.

· What to do when ... ·

...you feel *confused*

1 Corinthians 14:33
> For God is not the author of [a]confusion but of peace, as in all the churches of the saints.

2 Timothy 1:7
> For God has not given us a spirit of fear, but of power and of love and of a sound mind.

James 3:16-18
> For where envy and self-seeking exist, confusion and every evil thing are there. But the wisdom that is from above is first pure, then peaceable, gentle, willing to yield, full of mercy and good fruits, without partiality and without hypocrisy. Now the fruit of righteousness is sown in peace by those who make peace.

Isaiah 50:7
> "For the Lord God will help Me; Therefore I will not be disgraced; Therefore I have set My face like a flint, and I know that I will not be ashamed.

1 Peter 4:12-13
> Beloved, do not think it strange concerning the fiery trial which is to try you, as though some strange thing happened to you; but rejoice to the extent that you partake of Christ's sufferings, that when His glory is revealed, you may also be glad with exceeding joy.

Phillipians 4:6-7
> Be anxious for nothing, but in everything by prayer and supplication, with thanksgiving, let your requests be made known to God; and the peace of God, which surpasses all understanding, will guard your hearts and minds through Christ Jesus.

· What to do when ... ·

James 1:5
> If any of you lacks wisdom, let him ask of God, who gives to all liberally and without reproach, and it will be given to him.

Proverbs 3:5-6
> Trust in the Lord with all your heart, And lean not on your own understanding; In all your ways acknowledge Him, And He shall direct your paths.

Psalm 32:8
> I will instruct you and teach you in the way you should go; I will guide you with My eye.

Psalm 119:165
> Great peace have those who love Your law, And [a]nothing causes them to stumble.

Isaiah 43:2
> When you pass through the waters, I will be with you; And through the rivers, they shall not overflow you. When you walk through the fire, you shall not be burned, Nor shall the flame scorch you.

Isaiah 40:29
> He gives power to the weak, And to those who have no might He increases strength.

Isaiah 30:21
> Your ears shall hear a word behind you, saying, "This is the way, walk in it," Whenever you turn to the right hand or whenever you turn to the left.

· What to do when … ·

…you feel *tempted*

1 Corinthians 10:12-13
    Therefore let him who thinks he stands take heed lest he fall. No temptation has overtaken you except such as is common to man; but God is faithful, who will not allow you to be tempted beyond what you are able, but with the temptation will also make the way of escape, that you may be able to bear it.

Hebrews 4:14-16
    Seeing then that we have a great High Priest who has passed through the heavens, Jesus the Son of God, let us hold fast our confession. For we do not have a High Priest who cannot sympathize with our weaknesses, but was in all points tempted as we are, yet without sin. Let us therefore come boldly to the throne of grace, that we may obtain mercy and find grace to help in time of need.

Hebrews 2:18
    For in that He Himself has suffered, being tempted, He is able to aid those who are tempted.

2 Peter 2:9
    …then the Lord knows how to deliver the godly out of temptations and to reserve the unjust under punishment for the day of judgment,…

James 1:13-14
    Let no one say when he is tempted, "I am tempted by God"; for God cannot be tempted by evil, nor does He Himself tempt anyone. But each one is tempted when he is drawn away by his own desires and enticed.

· What to do when ... ·

Romans 6:14
> For sin shall not have dominion over you, for you are not under law but under grace.

Psalm 119:11
> Your word I have hidden in my heart, That I might not sin against You.

Proverbs 28:13
> He who covers his sins will not prosper, but whoever confesses and forsakes them will have mercy.

1 John 1:9
> If we confess our sins, He is faithful and just to forgive us our sins and to cleanse us from all unrighteousness.

1 Peter 5:8-9
> Be sober, be vigilant; because your adversary the devil walks about like a roaring lion, seeking whom he may devour. Resist him, steadfast in the faith, knowing that the same sufferings are experienced by your brotherhood in the world.

James 4:7
> Therefore submit to God. Resist the devil and he will flee from you.

1 John 4:4
> You are of God, little children, and have overcome them, because He who is in you is greater than he who is in the world.

· What to do when ... ·

...you feel *tempted*

Ephesians 6:10-22

> Finally, my brethren, be strong in the Lord and in the power of His might. Put on the whole armor of God, that you may be able to stand against the wiles of the devil. For we do not wrestle against flesh and blood, but against principalities, against powers, against the rulers of the darkness of this age, against spiritual hosts of wickedness in the heavenly places. Therefore take up the whole armor of God, that you may be able to withstand in the evil day, and having done all, to stand.
>
> Stand therefore, having girded your waist with truth, having put on the breastplate of righteousness, and having shod your feet with the preparation of the gospel of peace; above all, taking the shield of faith with which you will be able to quench all the fiery darts of the wicked one. And take the helmet of salvation, and the sword of the Spirit, which is the word of God; praying always with all prayer and supplication in the Spirit, being watchful to this end with all perseverance and supplication for all the saints — and for me, that utterance may be given to me, that I may open my mouth boldly to make known the mystery of the gospel, for which I am an ambassador in chains; that in it I may speak boldly, as I ought to speak.
>
> But that you also may know my affairs and how I am doing, Tychicus, a beloved brother and faithful minister in the Lord, will make all things known to you; whom I have sent to you for this very purpose, that you may know our affairs, and that he may comfort your hearts.

Jude 24-25
Now to Him who is able to keep you from stumbling, and to present you faultless before the presence of His glory with exceeding joy, to God our Savior, who alone is wise, be glory and majesty, dominion and power, both now and forever. Amen.

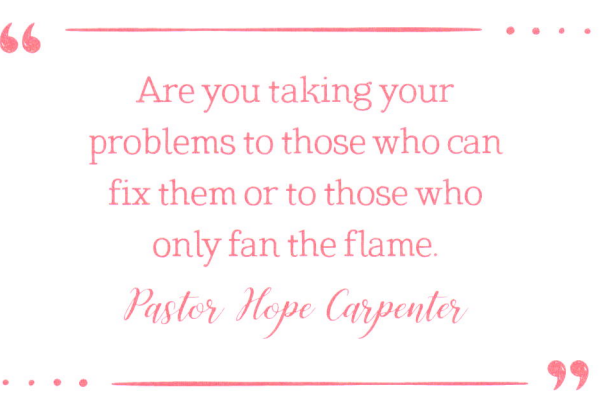

> Are you taking your problems to those who can fix them or to those who only fan the flame.
>
> *Pastor Hope Carpenter*

· What to do when ... ·
...you feel *rejected*

Psalm 37:5-7
    Commit your way to the Lord, Trust also in Him, and He shall bring it to pass. He shall bring forth your righteousness as the light, and your justice as the noonday. Rest in the Lord, and wait patiently for Him; Do not fret because of him who prospers in his way, because of the man who brings wicked schemes to pass.

Psalm 34:18
    The Lord is near to those who have a broken heart, and saves such as have a contrite spirit.

Romans 8:37
    Yet in all these things we are more than conquerors through Him who loved us.

Psalm 1:1-3
    Blessed is the man Who walks not in the counsel of the ungodly, nor stands in the path of sinners, nor sits in the seat of the scornful; But his delight is in the law of the Lord, And in His law he meditates day and night. He shall be like a tree planted by the rivers of water, That brings forth its fruit in its season, Whose leaf also shall not wither; And whatever he does shall prosper.

John 6:37
    All that the Father gives Me will come to Me, and the one who comes to Me I will by no means cast out.

· What to do when ... ·

Colossians 3:12-14
>Therefore, as the elect of God, holy and beloved, put on tender mercies, kindness, humility, meekness, longsuffering; bearing with one another, and forgiving one another, if anyone has a complaint against another; even as Christ forgave you, so you also must do. But above all these things put on love, which is the bond of perfection.

1 Samuel 16:7
>But the Lord said to Samuel, "Do not look at his appearance or at his physical stature, because I have refused him. For the Lord does not see as man sees; for man looks at the outward appearance, but the Lord looks at the heart."

1 Peter 4:16
>Yet if anyone suffers as a Christian, let him not be ashamed, but let him glorify God in this matter.

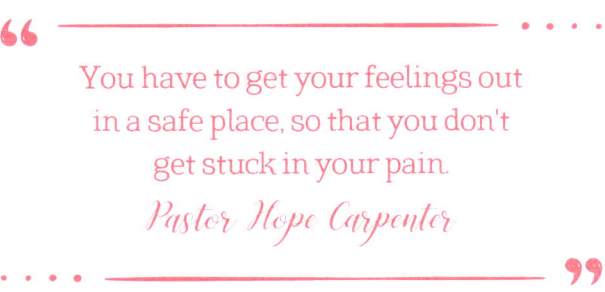

> "You have to get your feelings out in a safe place, so that you don't get stuck in your pain."
> — *Pastor Hope Carpenter*

· What to do when ... ·

...you feel *angry*

James 1:19-20
> So then, my beloved brethren, let every man be swift to hear, slow to speak, slow to wrath; for the wrath of man does not produce the righteousness of God.

Ephesians 4:26
> "Be angry, and do not sin": do not let the sun go down on your wrath,..."

Proverbs 15:1
> A soft answer turns away wrath, but a harsh word stirs up anger.

Matthew 6:14
> "For if you forgive men their trespasses, your heavenly Father will also forgive you."

Proverbs 14:29
> He who is slow to wrath has great understanding, but he who is impulsive exalts folly.

Proverbs 16:32
> He who is slow to anger is better than the mighty, and he who rules his spirit than he who takes a city.

Ecclesiastes 7:9
> Do not hasten in your spirit to be angry, For anger rests in the bosom of fools.

Romans 12:19
> Beloved, do not avenge yourselves, but rather give place to wrath; for it is written, "Vengeance is Mine, I will repay," says the Lord.

Psalm 37:8
> Cease from anger, and forsake wrath; Do not fret—it only causes harm.

· What to do when ... ·

Proverbs 25:21-22
>If your enemy is hungry, give him bread to eat; And if he is thirsty, give him water to drink; For so you will heap coals of fire on his head, and the Lord will reward you.

Hebrews 10:30
>For we know Him who said, "Vengeance is Mine, I will repay," says the Lord. And again, "The Lord will judge His people."

Ephesians 4:31-32
>Let all bitterness, wrath, anger, clamor, and evil speaking be put away from you, with all malice. And be kind to one another, tenderhearted, forgiving one another, even as God in Christ forgave you.

Matthew 5:22-24
>But I say to you that whoever is angry with his brother [a]without a cause shall be in danger of the judgment. And whoever says to his brother, 'Raca!' shall be in danger of the council. But whoever says, 'You fool!' shall be in danger of hell fire. Therefore if you bring your gift to the altar, and there remember that your brother has something against you, leave your gift there before the altar, and go your way. First be reconciled to your brother, and then come and offer your gift.

Proverbs 14:16-17
>A wise man fears and departs from evil, But a fool rages and is self-confident. A quick-tempered man acts foolishly, and a man of wicked intentions is hated.

· What to do when ... ·
...you feel *afraid*

2 Timothy 1:7
> For God has not given us a spirit of fear, but of power and of love and of a sound mind.

Romans 8:15-16
> For you did not receive the spirit of bondage again to fear, but you received the Spirit of adoption by whom we cry out, "Abba, Father." The Spirit Himself bears witness with our spirit that we are children of God,…

1 John 4:18
> There is no fear in love; but perfect love casts out fear, because fear involves torment. But he who fears has not been made perfect in love.

Psalm 91:1-2
> He who dwells in the secret place of the Most High shall abide under the shadow of the Almighty. I will say of the Lord, "He is my refuge and my fortress; My God, in Him I will trust."

Isaiah 40:31
> But those who wait on the Lord shall renew their strength; They shall mount up with wings like eagles, they shall run and not be weary, they shall walk and not faint.

Psalm 23:4-5
> Yea, though I walk through the valley of the shadow of death, I will fear no evil; For You are with me; Your rod and Your staff, they comfort me. You prepare a table before me in the presence of my enemies; You anoint my head with oil; My cup runs over.

· What to do when ... ·

Psalm 91:4-7
> He shall cover you with His feathers, And under His wings you shall take refuge; His truth shall be your shield and buckler. You shall not be afraid of the terror by night, Nor of the arrow that flies by day, Nor of the pestilence that walks in darkness, Nor of the destruction that lays waste at noonday. A thousand may fall at your side, and ten thousand at your right hand; But it shall not come near you.

Hebrews 13:6 & 8
> So we may boldly say: "The Lord is my helper; I will not fear. What can man do to me?" ... Jesus Christ is the same yesterday, today, and forever.

Psalm 91:10-11, 14
> No evil shall befall you, Nor shall any plague come near your dwelling; For He shall give His angels charge over you, to keep you in all your ways. ... "Because he has set his love upon Me, therefore I will deliver him; I will set him on high, because he has known My name.

Proverbs 3:25-26
> Do not be afraid of sudden terror, nor of trouble from the wicked when it comes; For the Lord will be your confidence, and will keep your foot from being caught.

Isaiah 54:14
> In righteousness you shall be established; You shall be far from oppression, for you shall not fear; And from terror, for it shall not come near you.

· What to do when ... ·

...you feel *afraid*

John 14:27

> Peace I leave with you, My peace I give to you; not as the world gives do I give to you. Let not your heart be troubled, neither let it be afraid.

Psalm 27:1, 3

> The Lord is my light and my salvation; Whom shall I fear? The Lord is the strength of my life; Of whom shall I be afraid? ... Though an army may encamp against me, My heart shall not fear; Though war may rise against me, In this I will be confident.

> Don't mistake God's protection for punishment. Everything that He does is because He loves you.
>
> *Pastor Hope Carpenter*

· What to do when ... ·

...you feel *sick*

Jeremiah 30:17
> For I will restore health to you And heal you of your wounds,' says the Lord, 'Because they called you an outcast saying: "This is Zion; No one seeks her." '

Jeremiah 17:14
> Heal me, O Lord, and I shall be healed; Save me, and I shall be saved, for You are my praise.

Isaiah 53:5
> But He was wounded for our transgressions, He was bruised for our iniquities; The chastisement for our peace was upon Him, And by His stripes we are healed.

Mark 16:17-18
> "And these signs will follow those who believe: In My name they will cast out demons; they will speak with new tongues; they will take up serpents; and if they drink anything deadly, it will by no means hurt them; they will lay hands on the sick, and they will recover."

James 5:14-15
> Is anyone among you sick? Let him call for the elders of the church, and let them pray over him, anointing him with oil in the name of the Lord. And the prayer of faith will save the sick, and the Lord will raise him up. And if he has committed sins, he will be forgiven.

Psalm 103:3
> Who forgives all your iniquities, Who heals all your diseases,...

· What to do when... ·

...you feel *sick*

Hebrews 13:8
>Jesus Christ is the same yesterday, today, and forever.

3 John 2
>Beloved, I pray that you may prosper in all things and be in health, just as your soul prospers.

Matthew 9:35
>Then Jesus went about all the cities and villages, teaching in their synagogues, preaching the gospel of the kingdom, and healing every sickness and every disease among the people.

Luke 6:19
>And the whole multitude sought to touch Him, for power went out from Him and healed them all.

1 Peter 2:24
>...who Himself bore our sins in His own body on the tree, that we, having died to sins, might live for righteousness—by whose [a]stripes you were healed.

Proverbs 4:20-22
>My son, give attention to my words; Incline your ear to my sayings. Do not let them depart from your eyes; Keep them in the midst of your heart; For they are life to those who find them, And health to all their flesh.

Psalm 107:20
>He sent His word and healed them, and delivered them from their destructions.

· What to do when ... ·

Exodus 15:26
> ...and said, "If you diligently heed the voice of the Lord your God and do what is right in His sight, give ear to His commandments and keep all His statutes, I will put none of the diseases on you which I have brought on the Egyptians. For I am the Lord who heals you."

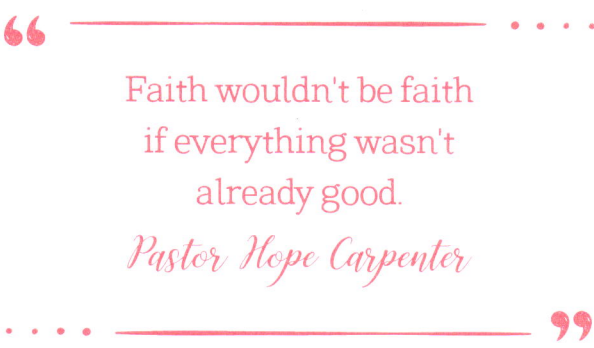

> Faith wouldn't be faith if everything wasn't already good.
> *Pastor Hope Carpenter*

· What to do when ... ·

...you feel *stressed*

Ecclesiastes 7:8-9
> The end of a thing is better than its beginning; The patient in spirit is better than the proud in spirit. Do not hasten in your spirit to be angry, for anger rests in the bosom of fools.

Hebrews 12:1
> Therefore we also, since we are surrounded by so great a cloud of witnesses, let us lay aside every weight, and the sin which so easily ensnares us, and let us run with endurance the race that is set before us,...

Hebrews 10:35-36
> Therefore do not cast away your confidence, which has great reward. For you have need of endurance, so that after you have done the will of God, you may receive the promise:...

Romans 15:4-5
> For whatever things were written before were written for our learning, that we through the patience and comfort of the Scriptures might have hope. Now may the God of patience and comfort grant you to be like-minded toward one another, according to Christ Jesus,...

Ephesians 4:2
> ...with all lowliness and gentleness, with longsuffering, bearing with one another in love,...

Romans 12:12
> ...rejoicing in hope, patient in tribulation, continuing steadfastly in prayer;...

· What to do when... ·

Hebrews 6:12
>that you do not become sluggish, but imitate those who through faith and patience inherit the promises.

Romans 8:25-26
>But if we hope for what we do not see, we eagerly wait for it with perseverance. Likewise the Spirit also helps in our weaknesses. For we do not know what we should pray for as we ought, but the Spirit Himself makes intercession for us with groanings which cannot be uttered.

Lamentations 3:25-26
>The Lord is good to those who wait for Him, To the soul who seeks Him. It is good that one should hope and wait quietly for the salvation of the Lord.

Psalm 27:14
>Wait on the Lord; Be of good courage, and He shall strengthen your heart; Wait, I say, on the Lord!

Galations 5:22-23
>But the fruit of the Spirit is love, joy, peace, longsuffering, kindness, goodness, faithfulness, gentleness, self-control. Against such there is no law.

Psalm 37:7-8, 16
>Rest in the Lord, and wait patiently for Him; Do not fret because of him who prospers in his way, Because of the man who brings wicked schemes to pass. Cease from anger, and forsake wrath; Do not fret—it only causes harm.
>... A little that a righteous man has is better than the riches of many wicked.

· What to do when ... ·
...you feel *stressed*

Psalm 40:1
> I waited patiently for the Lord; And He inclined to me, and heard my cry

Romans 5:3-5
> And not only that, but we also glory in tribulations, knowing that tribulation produces perseverance; and perseverance, character; and character, hope. Now hope does not disappoint, because the love of God has been poured out in our hearts by the Holy Spirit who was given to us.

James 1:2-4
> My brethren, count it all joy when you fall into various trials, knowing that the testing of your faith produces patience. But let patience have its perfect work, that you may be perfect and complete, lacking nothing.

James 5:7-8
> Therefore be patient, brethren, until the coming of the Lord. See how the farmer waits for the precious fruit of the earth, waiting patiently for it until it receives the early and latter rain. You also be patient. Establish your hearts, for the coming of the Lord is at hand.

> " Problems are a key to your promotion.
> Stop running from problems and let them build you.
> — *Pastor Hope Carpenter*

The next time you feel like God can't use you, just remember:

- Noah was a drunk
- Abraham was too old
- Isaac was a daydreamer
- Jacob was a liar
- Joseph was abused
- Moses stuttered
- Gideon was afraid
- Samsom had long hair and was a womanizer
- Rahab was a prostitute
- Jeremiah and Timothy were too young
- David had an affair and was a murderer
- Elijah was suicidal
- Isaiah preached naked
- Jonah ran from God
- Naomi was a widow
- Job went bankrupt
- Peter denied Christ
- The Disciples fell asleep while praying
- Martha worried about everything
- The Samaritan woman was divorced, more than once
- Zaccheus was too small
- Paul was too religious
- Timothy had an ulcer
- And Lazarus was dead!

Now! No more excuses! God can use you to your full potential.
Besides, you aren't the message, you are just the messenger.

— *Author Unknown*

> Surround yourself with people who can pray you out of a bad situation instead of get you into one.
> *Pastor Hope Carpenter*

recipes

> "
>
> A recipe has no soul.
> You as the cook must bring
> soul to the recipe.
>
> "
>
> Thomas Keller

· Recipes | Appetizers ·

Nana Cindy's Salsa
by Cynthia Lara

I've been married for almost 42 years. My family, especially my husband Gilbert loves my cooking. Even his ushers always ask me to make my homemade salsa.

Ingredients:
- 10 ripe fresh tomatoes, chopped
- 2 large cans petite diced tomatoes
- 2 large bunch cilantro, chopped
- 2 or 3 bunches of green onion
- 6 cloves of fresh garlic, minced
- Juice of 1 lemon
- Garlic salt, pepper and salt to taste
- 10 roasted fresh jalapeno, chopped

» Simply chop and mix together. I use chopper shears from Pampered Chef — love them! Refrigerate. Enjoy!

You can also make an amazing bean dip!

Ingredients:
- Large can of spicy jalapeno Rosarita refried beans
- 1 cup of shredded cheese
- 1 cup Nana Cindy's Salsa

» In microwave-safe bowl mix refried beans, cheese and my salsa. Heat in microwave for 3-4 minutes, stir. So amazing!

Of course, lots of tortilla chips!

Recipes | Appetizers

Creamy Avocado Dip
by Autumn Owen

Ingredients:
- 2 large avocados
- Juice of 1 lemon
- ½ tsp garlic powder
- 1 package cream cheese
- ½ of an onion, finely chopped
- salt (amount according to taste)

» Mix all ingredients together until creamy! (KitchenAid mixer works great!) Serve with tortilla chips and enjoy!

Easy-Peel Boiled Eggs
by Sandra Lee

» In a pot, boil some water, enough to totally submerge the eggs you're gonna cook.

» Set the eggs you're going to cook in a bowl of warm water.

» When the pot of water starts to boil, turn the stove off. Gently spoon your eggs one by one into the hot water.

» Cover and let the water and eggs cool for several hours. I usually let the water cool to about room temperature.

» When cooled, the eggs are perfectly hard boiled and the shell peels off very easy.

Tip: Think ahead, the work is easy but the process is slow, the end results are perfect eggs.

· Recipes | Appetizers ·

Fried Lobster Bites
by Chanlin Carpenter Guthrie

I have made this appetizer on a few different occasions at my house and they're so good, no one saves me any before I'm done cooking! They are gone in a few minutes every time and I promise that any seafood lover is bound to die for this dish.

PRO TIP:
When frying food's, set out your meat and cool it down to a room temp. If you add cold food to hot oil, it will cause the food to be unevenly cooked, the outside will be burnt, and the meat will be be tough.

Ingredients:
- 4 lobster tails
- 1 tbsp Old Bay seasoning
- Salt and pepper to taste
- Oil
- 1 pack Louisiana fish fry batter (cajun if you prefer a little spice)
- Cocktail sauce/tartar sauce

» Heat Oil in a large pan (enough to fill the bottom of pan) on medium/high heat but not too high or you will have oil popping everywhere!

» Cut open lobster tail and pull the meat out. Cut the meat into little "bite" size pieces.

» Put batter, salt and pepper in a small bowl and coat the lobster bites thoroughly.

» Add coated Lobster Bites to the oil and cook until a golden brown crust has formed.

» Dry the oil off on a plate covered with a paper towel then transfer to an appetizer tray. Dip in Preferred sauce and you have a crowd pleasing appetizer!

· Recipes | Appetizers ·

Beef Empanadas
by Chanlin Carpenter Guthrie

Ingredients:
- 1 pack Goya Empanada dough
- 1 lb ground beef
- 1 white onion diced
- 3 tbsp of cumin
- 3 tbsp of Adobo seasoning
- Salt and pepper
- 1 egg
- 3 cloves of garlic minced
- 1 tbsp of dried oregano
- 1 bunch of fresh cilantro chopped
- 2 tbsp butter

» Add butter to pan and add onion. Let cook until transparent then add the garlic.

» Add ground beef, cumin, dried oregano, Adobo, salt and pepper. Let the meat cook and once there is no more raw meat, add the cilantro. Let the flavors mix for a while on a simmer, then set filling aside in a bowl.

» Lay out the dough disks and put a generous spoonful of the filling in the center of the disk. Close dough using a fork. You can look up a video for step-by-step instructions on closing an Empanada if you're struggling (no shame).

» If you have time, put empanadas in the fridge to help them seal and to prevent any leaking.

» Pre-heat the oven to 400° F (200C) for medium sized empanadas, or 375F (190F) for smaller empanadas.

» Place the empanadas on baking sheet, lightly greased or lined with parchment paper.

» Brush the empanadas with the whisked egg mix; this will give a nice golden glow when baked.

» Bake the empanadas at 400F for 20 minutes, or until golden on top.

» Serve warm, alone or with your choice of dipping sauce.

· Recipes | Appetizers ·

Baked Brie
by Neena Troxell

Ingredients:
- Brie wheel
- Puff pastry sheet
- Fruit preserves (I recommend Fig or peach, or even plain honey)
- Optional: sliced almonds or any nut that your prefer

» Preheat the oven to 400°.

» Cut puff pastry sheet into a square that will fit your brie wheel.

» Place puff pastry sheet onto a baking tray and place brie on top of the puff pastry.

» Spread your preserves or honey on the top of the brie wheel. Add nuts to your preference.

» Fold the puff pastry over the cheese to enclose it until it is all covered.

» Bake for 25 to 30 minutes and cool before serving.

» Serve with apples, crackers or a baguette.

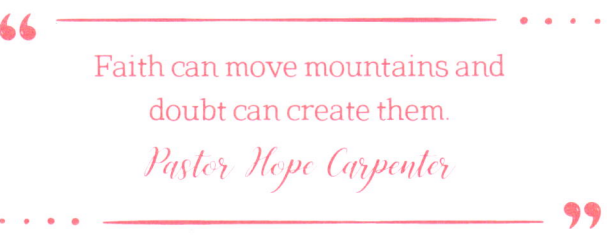

> Faith can move mountains and doubt can create them.
> *Pastor Hope Carpenter*

· Recipes | Appetizers ·

Creamy Avocado Dip
by Autumn Owen

Ingredients:
- 2 large avocados
- Juice of 1 lemon
- ½ tsp garlic powder
- 1 package cream cheese
- ½ of an onion, finely chopped
- Salt (amount according to taste)

» Mix all ingredients together until creamy! (KitchenAid mixer works great!) Serve with tortilla chips and enjoy!

Easy-Peel Boiled Eggs
by Sandra Lee

» In a pot, boil some water, enough to totally submerge the eggs you're gonna cook.

» Set the eggs you're going to cook in a bowl of warm water.

» When the pot of water starts to boil, turn the stove off. Gently spoon your eggs one by one into the hot water.

» Cover and let the water and eggs cool for several hours. I usually let the water cool to about room temperature.

» When cooled, the eggs are perfectly hard boiled and the shell peels off very easy.

Tip: Think ahead, the work is easy but the process is slow, the end results are perfect eggs.

· Recipes | Appetizers ·

Turkey Pepper Jack Rolls
by Hope Carpenter

Ingredients:
    – 8 oz can crescent rolls
    – 8 slices deli turkey
    – 4 oz shredded pepper jack cheeseor slices
    – 2 tbsp unsalted buttermelted
    – 1 tsp yellow mustard
    – ½ tbsp poppy seeds

» Preheat oven to 375°. Line a baking sheet with parchment paper.

» Stir mustard into the melted butter and set aside.

» Fold a slice of turkey in half and place it on the wide end of the crescent. Top turkey with about a tablespoon of shredded pepper jack cheese. Roll up the crescent and place on baking sheet. Repeat for all crescent rolls and bake for 11-13 minutes, or until golden brown.

» Remove crescents from oven and transfer to a cooling rack. Brush with butter and mustard mixture then immediately sprinkle with poppy seeds. It's best to work in batches of 2 or 3 so the butter does not begin to harden before you can add the topping.

» Serve warm.

Recipes | Appetizers

Easy Cheezy Pizza Dip
by Hope Carpenter

Ingredients:
- 8 oz softened Cream Cheese
- 1 tsp dried Basil
- 2 tsp dried Oregano
- ½ cup grated Parmesan Cheese
- 2 cup grated Mozzarella Cheese
- 1¼ cup Pizza Sauce
- 14 slices Pepperoni

» Preheat oven to 375°.

» Spray a pie baking dish with non-stick spray.

» Add basil and oregano to Cream Cheese and mix until blended.

» Spread Cream Cheese in bottom of prepared dish.

» Sprinkle ¼ cup Parmesan over dish.

» Sprinkle 1 cup Mozzarella over dish.

» Evenly pour pizza sauce to cover mixture.

» Sprinkle remaining Parmesan over sauce.

» Sprinkle remaining Mozzarella over dish.

» Top with pepperoni slices.

» Bake for about 25 minutes or until cheese has melted.

> Learn to laugh …
> It drives the devil insane
> and heals what
> troubles you.
> *Pastor Hope Carpenter*

· Recipes | Side Dishes ·

Summer Squash Casserole
by Hope Carpenter

Ingredients:
- 1 1/2 lb fresh yellow summer squash, thinly sliced
- 1 medium, fresh onion, finely chopped
- 1 tbsp water
- 2 medium fresh carrots, coarsely shredded
- 1 (18.5 oz) can chicken corn chowder
- 1 (8 oz) bag shredded sharp cheddar cheese, divided
- 1/4 tsp kosher salt
- 1/4 tsp pepper
- 1 (3.5 oz) stick herb garlic butter
- 2 cups cornbread stuffing mix
- 2 tbsp cooked bacon pieces

» Preheat oven to 400°. Slice squash and chop onion (1 cup). Combine squash, onions, and water in microwave-safe bowl; microwave on HIGH for 7-8 minutes or until tender. Meanwhile, shred carrots.

» Drain squash very thoroughly in colander. Combine squash mixture, chowder, carrots, 1 cup cheese. Salt, and pepper until blended.

» Melt butter in microwave, combine with stuffing mix. Place one-half of the stuffing in bottom of 2 quart baking dish. Top with squash mixture.

» Stir remaining 1 cup cheese and bacon into other half of stuffing; spread over squash layer. Bake 15-20 minutes or until topping is crisp and brown and sauce bubbles around edge of dish. Serve.

Recipes | Side Dishes

Cabbage Salad
by Tamaya Lee

Ingredients:
- 1 cup of sliced almonds
- 3 - 10 oz. pkgs. shredded angel hair cole slaw
- 3 - 3 oz. pkgs. chicken flavor Top Ramen noodles
- 8 green onions
- 2 tbsp sugar
- ½ cup corn oil
- 4 tbsp rice vinegar
- 1 tsp pepper

» Sauté 1 cup of sliced almonds in a little butter. Add 3 packs of shredded angel hair cole slaw and sliced green onions.

» Crush 3 packages of chicken flavor Top Ramen noodles and add to cabbage mixture.

» For dressing, mix together in container or blender sugar, oil, rice vinegar, and 2 flavor packets from the chicken Top Ramen soup, and 1 tsp of pepper.

» Pour dressing over cabbage mix when ready to eat.

» If you're taking salad to a park or somewhere else, place almonds, cole slaw, onions, and crushed chicken noodles in separate bags to keep crunchy. Bring large bowl to mix everything in. Add dressing just before you're ready to eat.

· Recipes | Side Dishes ·

Taco Salad
by Monica Leyba

Ingredients:
- 1 lb ground beef
- 4 diced tomatoes
- 1 red onion in half slices
- 1 can sliced black olives
- 1 bag or head of lettuce
- 1 large bag of Doritos nacho chips
- 1 packet of taco seasoning
- 4 diced avocados
- 1 can dark kidney beans
- 1 bag shredded cheddar cheese
- 16 oz. Catalina salad dressimg

» Brown 1 lb. ground beef with taco seasoning packet and let cool.

» In large bowl, mix vegetables, beans, cheese and crushed Doritos nacho chips.

» Pour and mix Catalina salad dressing (about half a bottle to taste but don't put on until ready to serve so it doesn't get soggy)

Post Exercise Reload – Omega3 Rich Salmon Rice Cake
by Sandra Lee

Ingredients:
- Laughing cow cheese
- Trader Joe's pastrami smoked salmon
- 1 cinnamon sugar rice cake

» Spread the cheese on top of rice cake, add sliced salmon on top.

· Recipes | Side Dishes ·

Southern Green Beans
by Hope Carpenter

Ingredients:
- 2-3 large cans green beans
- 1 pack of Splenda
- Salt and pepper
- 2 tbsp of vegetable oil
- 1 piece of fat back or ham hock
- 1 onion, sliced
- 2 cups of water

» Add all ingredients and boil in medium high heat for one hour, adding some water if needed!!!! Enjoy

> Note to self: Choose JOY!
>
> *Pastor Hope Carpenter*

· Recipes | Side Dishes ·

Broccoli & Cheese Casserole
by Hope Carpenter

Ingredients:
- 3 heads broccoli, cut into florets (about 8 cups)
- ½ cup butter
- ½ cup all-purpose flour
- 2 cups whole milk or heavy cream
- ½ tsp Kosher salt
- ½ tsp ground black or white pepper
- ⅛ tsp cayenne pepper
- 1 cup grated Monterey Jack cheese
- 1 cup sour cream
- 1 cup grated Cheddar cheese
- 2 cups crushed buttery crackers

» Preheat oven to 350° F. Spray a 13x9 inch baking dish with nonstick cooking spray.

» Add broccoli florets to a large heavy-bottomed stockpot of boiling water. Cook for 3-5 minutes and then drain broccoli from the water. Set aside.

» Melt butter over medium, heat in a small saucepan. Whisk in flour until well-combined, then whisk in milk, salt, pepper, cayenne pepper and 1 cup of Monterey Jack cheese. Reduce heat to simmer and continue to whisk until sauce simmers slightly around the edges and has thickened slightly. Stir in sour cream.

» Arrange broccoli in casserole dish and then pour cream sauce over broccoli. Top with cheddar cheese and crushed crackers.

» Bake uncovered for 35-40 minutes. Serve

· Recipes | Side Dishes ·

Best Coleslaw Ever
by Sandy Hutchins

Ingredients:
- 1 bag of shredded coleslaw (I like the different colors of cabbage)
- 1 medium apple (I use a red/green one to make it cute)
- ½ cup of dried cranberries or raisins
- 1 jar of Marie's Poppy Seed Dressing

» In large bowl toss cabbage, diced apples, cranberries or raisins.

» The key to your slaw is the dressing. So buy a jar of Marie's Poppy Seed Dressing NOT the coleslaw dressing. It's sold right by the salads and your bag of coleslaw in your larger grocery stores. Just add to your liking & consistency.

» You will find that people who didn't like coleslaw before, will LOVE your coleslaw. It's all because of Marie's Poppy Seed Dressing. Enjoy!

Making Gravy
by Dona Flores

Ingredients:
- 1 tbsp butter
- 1 tbsp flour
- 1 cup chicken or beef stock

» Mash soft butter into flour and make a paste. Melt it in the pan add 1 cup of chicken or beef stock drippings. Season to taste. Easy peasy. Works every time!

· Recipes | Side Dishes ·

Breakfast Potatoes
by Leslie Norman

Ingredients:
- 2 or however many frozen shredded hashbrowns
- 12 eggs
- 1 extra large bag of shredded Mexican blend cheese
- 1 can of cream of mushroom soup (low sodium)
- 1 can of cream of celery soup (low sodium)
- 2 packages of flavored sausages
  (maple brown sugar or Vermont maple syrup sausages)
- 1 package of Johnsonville Applewood smoked bacon
- 1½ tspn of lemon pepper
- 1 stock of green onions
- 1 baking pan such as the size of baking a turkey
- Bakers butter that is soften so the eggs and cheese don't stick

» Preheat oven to 395°.

» Cut up all the meats and green onions to be mixed in the potatoes.

» Warm the cream of mushroom and cream of celery soups to mix well with all ingredients.

» Pour potatoes in pan, make sure they are broken up. Add cheese and meats first, then mix in the soups slowly. Add the eggs to the mixture then add more cheeses.

» Once all mixed together, smooth out the top add cheese to the top .

» Cover with foil and cook until the eggs are completely done in the center of mixture. Half way through remove the foil and cook through add more cheese for a crust.

· Recipes | Side Dish ·

Quick & Easy Eggs
by Daisy Gutierrez

Ingredients:
- Coconut baking spray
- 2 eggs
- 1 avocado
- ½ green onion, sliced
- 3 cherry tomatoes, sliced

» Crack two eggs on the pan after spraying the pan with coconut baking spray. Cook the egg as you like then add the green onions and sliced tomatoes. Flip to cook on each side. Add slices of avocado and BAM!! There is your delicious eggs!

Homemade Sofrito
by Aisha Brady

Ingredients:
- 2 bunches cilantro
- 1 large Spanish yellow onion
- 1 red pepper
- 8-10 cloves of garlic
- 1 green pepper
- 8-10 ajicito peppers (Optional)

» With food processor or blender completely blend onions and garlic first. Add peppers and cilantro. Blend all ingredients completely, add small amounts of extra virgin olive oil, if necessary to make it smooth.

» Save in glass jars with tight lids in refrigerator up to 2 weeks or freeze in ice cube trays and store in zip lock bags.

» Add sofrito to your favorite soups, beans, marinades as a fresh and natural mix of herbs and vegetables providing lots of flavor to all of your favorite dishes.

· Recipes | Side Dish ·

Macaroni & Cheese
by Cindy Hayes

Ingredients:
- 16 oz box of macaroni elbow noodles
- 2 lbs Sharp shredded cheese
- 32 oz cottage cheese
- 16 oz sour cream
- 1 egg
- Salt & pepper to taste

» Cook noodles then drain and put in a LARGE bowl. Stir in 1 egg, and salt & pepper to taste. Mix well. Then start adding cottage cheese, a little at a time, and mix well until you use all of it. Add sour cream, a little at a time, mix in well until you use all of it. Start adding the shredded cheese, a little at a time mixing well and as you go.

» Once all of it is mixed well throughout the noodles, dump into a 9x12 pan.

» Cook for 30 min. Oven times may vary, but you want the cheese to be melted throughout. Ready to serve!

Corn Bake
by Sue Mase

Ingredients:
- 1 small onion cut up
- ½ cup butter
- 1 can whole corn
- 1 box Jiffy corn muffin mix
- 1 cup grated cheese (cheddar preferred)
- ½ bell pepper cut up
- 1 can cream style corn
- 3 eggs
- 1 cup sour cream

» Sauté onion and green pepper and butter. Mix together corn, eggs and jiffy corn muffin mix. Add to cooked vegetables. Pour into a large baking dish top with sour cream and grated cheese. Bake at 350° for approximately one hour or until golden brown serves 8 to 10.

· Recipes | Side Dish ·

Krishna's Indulgent Baked Mac and Cheese
by Krishna Sewal-Sandoval

Ingredients:

Sauce
- 1 cup whole milk
- ½ cup heavy cream
- ½ tsp mustard powder
- ¼ tsp cayenne pepper

Cornstarch Slurry
- 1 tbsp cornstarch
- 2 tbsp of water

Cheeses
- 8 oz. Cream cheese, room temperature, cut into pieces
- 8 oz. medium Cheddar cheese, shredded (about 2½ cups)
- 8 oz Muenster cheese, shredded (about 2 cups)
- 3 oz. Fontina cheese, shredded (about 1 cup)

Pasta
- 1 lb. of elbow macaroni
- 1 tbsp/15 g unsalted butter (or 2 tsp oil)
- Kosher salt

Topping
- 40g of panko breadcrumbs
- 2 tbsp/30 g unsalted butter
- ¼ tsp salt

Optional: Shredded romano, asiago & parmesan cheese blend

· Recipes | Side Dish ·

- Simmer milk, cream, mustard powder, and cayenne in a medium pot over medium heat, stirring and being careful not to let mixture boil, until heated through and well combined, 6–8 minutes.

- Mix cornstarch and 2 tbsp. water in a small bowl to make a slurry, then whisk into milk mixture. Bring to a boil and cook, whisking constantly, until mixture thickens, 1–2 minutes.

- Add cream cheese and cook, whisking occasionally, until mixture is smooth and thick, 2–3 minutes.

- Reduce heat to medium-low and gradually stir in Cheddar, Muenster, and Fontina. Cook, stirring occasionally and reducing heat if mixture starts to boil, until cheeses are almost melted (it's okay if you see a few shreds of unmelted cheese), 4–6 minutes.

- Meanwhile, cook pasta in a large pot of boiling salted water, stirring occasionally, until according to instructions on box. Drain and stir into cheese mixture. Gently stir until sauce is smooth and creamy and pasta is evenly coated; taste and season with salt, if needed.

- If you want it a little thinner, add a little more milk. Don't make it too thin!

- Remove from heat and transfer onto baking dish.

- Sprinkle panko breadcrumbs and shredded romano, asiago & parmesan cheese spread to cover the dish.

- Bake for 25 minutes or until top is light golden. Serve immediately.

> God doesn't have one bad day planned for you.
> — *Pastor Hope Carpenter*

· Recipes | Side Dish ·

Potato Salad
by Catherine Belardo

Ingredients:
- 5-6 medium-size potatoes
- 8 large eggs
- ½ cup of Best Foods Real Mayonnaise
- 1 carrot, finely chopped
- 1 celery stock, finely chopped
- ½ onion, finely chopped
- Salt and pepper to taste

» Bring a large pot of salted water to a boil. Add potatoes and cook until tender but still firm, about 15 minutes. Drain, cool, peel and dice.

» Place eggs in a saucepan and cover with cold water. Bring water to a boil; cover, remove from heat, and let eggs stand in hot water for 10 to 12 minutes. Remove from hot water, cool, peel and chop.

» In a large bowl, combine the potatoes, eggs, celery, onion, salt, pepper and mayonnaise. Mix together well and refrigerate until chilled.

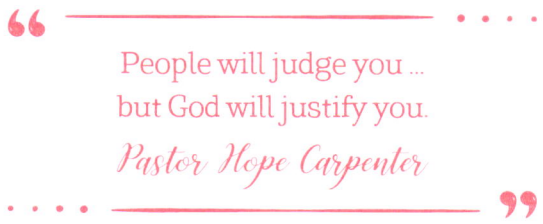

> People will judge you ...
> but God will justify you.
>
> *Pastor Hope Carpenter*

· Recipes | Main Dish ·

Crock Pot Fajitas
by Hope Carpenter

Ingredients:
- 2 lbs boneless skinless chicken breast halves
- 1 (14.5 oz) can petite diced tomatoes with green chilies
- 1 red, orange and green bell pepper, julienned
- 1 large yellow onion, halved and sliced
- 4 cloves garlic, minced
- 2½ tsp chili powder
- 2 tsp ground cumin
- 1 tsp paprika
- ¾ tsp ground coriander
- 1 tsp salt
- ¾ tsp pepper
- 2 tbsp fresh lime juice
- 1 tbsp honey

For serving:
- 12 6-inch flour tortillas
- Sour cream, cilantro, salsa, guacamole, monterey jack or cheddar cheese

Instructions:

» Pour half of the canned tomatoes into the bottom of a slow cooker and spread into an even layer. Top with half of the peppers and half of the onions. Sprinkle garlic in. Top with chicken breasts.

» In a bowl whisk together chili powder, cumin, paprika, coriander, salt and pepper. Evenly sprinkle half of the seasoning over chicken breasts then flip chicken and sprinkle in remainder. Top with remaining half of the tomatoes, then layer in remaining peppers and onions.

- » Cover and cook on HIGH heat 3 - 4 hours or low heat 6 - 8 hours, until chicken has cooked through and veggies are tender (note that if you want to be able to cut chicken into strips cook more near lesser time on HIGH or LOW, otherwise it will probably just shred, which is also fine).
- » Remove chicken, and cut into strips, or shred. Ladle out 1 cup of the broth in slow cooker (mostly tomato liquid) and discard.
- » In a small bowl whisk together lime juice and honey and add to slow cooker along with chicken and season with additional salt to taste if desired. Gently toss. Serve warm in warmed tortillas with sour cream and optional guacamole, cheese and salsa.

Pot Roast
by Hope Carpenter

Ingredients:
- Chuck Roast
- 1 cup water
- 1 can cream of mushroom soup
- 1 pack of lipton onion soup mix
- As many carrots as you like
- 1 cup chopped celery
- Salt and pepper

Directions: Put all ingredients over chuck roast and cook on low for 12 hours.

· Recipes | Main Dish ·

Garlic Butter Shrimp
by Hope Carpenter

Ingredients:
- 1 pound shrimp, peeled and deveined
- 6 tbsp butter, divided
- 1/2 tsp kosher salt
- 1/2 tsp black pepper
- 5 garlic cloves, minced
- 1/2 cup chicken stock
- 1/4 tsp red pepper flakes
- 2 tbsp lemon juice
- 2 tbsp minced parsely

Instructions:

» Heat 2 tablespoons of butter in a large heavy bottomed skillet over medium heat.

» Add the shrimp to the skillet and sprinkle with salt and pepper.

» Cook, stirring occasionally, for 4-5 minutes or until shrimp is cooked through.

» Remove shrimp to a plate and set aside.

» Add the garlic to the skillet ad cook, stirring constantly, for 30 seconds

» Add the chicken stock and whisk to combine. Simmer until stock has reduced by half about 5-10 minutes.

» Add the remaining 4 tablespoons of butter, lemon juice, and red pepper to the sauce. Stir to melt the butter and cook for 2 more minutes.

» Remove from the heat and return the shrimp to the sauce. Sprinkle the parsley over the top and stir to combine.

» Serve immediately.

· Recipes | Main Dish ·

Kielbasa Sausage and Parmesan Noodles
by Yasi Figueroa

Ingredients:
- 1 bag of wide egg noodles
- 1 pack of kielbasa sausage
- Salt and pepper (the amount and flavor is up to you)
- Parmesan (grated)
- 1 stick of butter (unsalted)

» Cook the noodles as directed on the package. Drain noodles and set aside.

» Cut kielbasa sausage in half then in sixths then cook thoroughly in skillet.

» Take pot of noodles and mix in 1 stick of butter until fully melted, add salt and pepper (to taste) and about 15 shakes of parmesan.

» Stir-in cooked kielbasa and enjoy!

Oven Roasted Tri-Tip
by Christine Corpus

» Pre-heat oven to 425 degrees.

» Using untrimmed tri-tip roast. (If untrimmed on both sides, trim one side) Rub tri-tip with your favorite seasoning salt.

» Heat oil in an oven safe pan on stove top and sear tri-tip, fat side down (about 4 minutes or until we'll-seared). Flip roast over and put in oven.

» Bake for 10-15 minutes per pound (12 minutes gives a perfect medium-rare).

» Allow roast to rest for 10 minutes.

· Recipes | Main Dish ·

Moe's Spicy White Sauce Pasta
by Brendan Moe

Ingredients:
- Baby spinach
- 1 package thick linguine noodles
- 1 lb. ground beef or meat of choice
- 1-2 tbsp butter
- ½ tsp pepper
- 8 oz./16 oz. milk
- ½ tsp salt
- ½ tsp red pepper
- ½ tbsp minced garlic clove

Pasta & Spinach Prep:

» Layer on plates a large bed of baby spinach, then linguine noodles cooked al dente. Layer cooked ground beef, or meat of choice.

Spicy White Sauce: *One batch should feed 2-3 people. For super spicy use first measurements, less spicy use second measurements.*

» In a small saucepan, on medium heat one/two tablespoons of butter. Add one/two tablespoons of white flour. Simmer until tan and bubbly, quickly add 8oz./16oz. milk. Stir constantly with a wire whisk on the bottom of pan.

» As soon as it starts to simmer, adjust heat to low. Add in ½ teaspoon of salt and black pepper, 1 teaspoon/½ teaspoon of ground ginger, ½ teaspoon of crushed red pepper seasoned to taste. Last ingredient for best taste: 1 tablespoon of freshly minced garlic clove.

» After sauce thickens, pour it over spinach, linguine noodles, and meat. Further optional enhancement is to dash a bit of ground nutmeg over the top.

· Recipes | Main Dish ·

Homemade Sloppy Joes
by Julie Warren

Ingredients:
- 1 tsp onion powder
- ¾ cup ketchup
- ¼ cup BBQ sauce
- 1 tbsp vinegar
- 1 tbsp yellow mustard
- 1 lb. ground turkey/beef
- 1 tbsp white sugar (1-2 tbsp simple syrup works perfectly as well)

» Preheat oven to 350°.

» Cook and drain meat.

» In separate bowl mix all other ingredients. Mix sauce in with the meat and simmer, if desired. You can simply mix the meat into the sauce and serve it up!

- -

Grits Casserole
by Elder Mary Locke

Ingredients:
- Grits – cooked (I use 6½ cups water and 1½ cups grits)
- 1 bell pepper (chopped)
- 1 medium onion (chopped)
- 1 package regular sausage w/sage and turkey sausage
- 1 package shredded mild cheddar cheese
- 2 cans cream of chicken soup
- Salt & pepper to taste

» Cook sausage, onion, and bell pepper together. Drain then add cream of chicken soup. Cook for 15 minutes on medium heat. Add to grits and mix then add cheese.

Bon appetite!!

· Recipes | Main Dish ·

Lemon Pepper Chicken Over Asparagus
by Chanlin Carpenter Guthrie

Ingredients:
- Chicken breasts (1-2 per person)
- 1 bunch of asparagus spears
- 3 cloves of garlic
- 1 lemon
- Oregano
- Salt & pepper
- Original Mrs. Dash

» Preheat oven to 400°.
» Cut asparagus and place in a large bowl and coat with olive oil, salt and pepper, and with 1 clove of garlic minced.
» Place asparagus in the bottom of a Pyrex pan.
» Put Chicken breasts on top of the asparagus and coat on both sides with seasonings and the rest of the garlic.
» Top off lemon juice (to preferred taste) and lay lemon slices on top of chicken.
» Put in oven for about 25-30 minutes. Make sure the chicken is thoroughly cooked. Eat and enjoy!

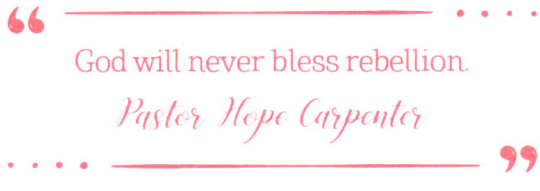

" God will never bless rebellion.
Pastor Hope Carpenter "

Recipes | Main Dish

Best Chicken or Pork Adobo – Ever!
by Anjeanette Marstadt

Ingredients:
- 2 lbs of chicken or pork
- ¼ soy sauce
- 10 pcs of whole black peppercorn
- 10 whole clove of garlic chopped
- ½ cup vinegar (apple cider)
- 1 tsp black pepper
- 1-2 bay leaves

» Fry chicken or pork pieces until brown. Add soy sauce, vinegar, pepper corn, and bay leaves to pot and boil for 10 minutes. Simmer until tender for 45 minutes to one hour on low.

Waffle Fried Chicken
by Laila Rigueroa

Ingredients:
- ¼ cup waffle mix
- ½ cup flour
- ½ cup corn meal
- ½ tsp garlic
- Pepper to taste
- Cayenne pepper to taste
- Salt to taste

» Heat peanut oil to 400°.

» Soak wingettes in 1 tbsp lemon juice, a pinch of red pepper flakes, 1 tbsp sugar, ½ cup water over night (you can substitute water with milk) the milk will make batter more cake-like.

» Take the wingettes out of the brine.

» Mix all dry ingredients and place in a bag, put the wings in the bag and shake.

» Fry until done.

· Recipes | Main Dish ·

Fun Individual Pizza
by Carla Johnson

Ingredients:
- Pillsbury Buttermilk Biscuits 6 to 8 piece per pack (buy as many as you need to feed per person)
- Marinara sauce, size depends on how many pizzas you want to make. One 16 to 24 oz jar might be enough for 12 to 24 mini pizzas.
- Shredded cheese of your choice (mozzarella preferred)
- Personal favorite toppings ie: Pepperoni, olives, peppers, tomatoes, pineapple, etc.

» Great for kids and teens or an adult gathering! Let them make it! Press out the biscuit to as round as you can make it without ripping it, just like a pizza. Add sauce and cheese and then your favorite toppings, but don't over stuff top.

» Preheat oven to 400 degrees, cook until the edges are light/medium brown and cheese is melted. Maybe about 15 to 24 minutes depending on your oven. Use cookie pan, or large pizza pan with 2 inches between each pizza.

Enjoy your personal pizza!

Quick Potluck Dish – Crock-Pot Lasagna
by Lissa Cato

» Buy a frozen lasagna put in the fridge. Next day, cut in pieces and put in crock-pot. Take to potluck and put on high and eat when ready! Fast and easy.

Emergency Meatball Chicken Soup
by Cindy Tapia

This recipe is for an emergency chicken soup. When your kid, neighbor, friend or loved one needs some TLC.

Ingredients:

Meatballs
- ½ lb. ground chicken breast or turkey
- ¼ cup of rolled oats or quick oats.
- 1 organic egg
- ½ small tomatoes chopped
- ⅛ small onion chopped
- 6 springs of cilantro chopped
- Pinch of salt

Soup
- ½ onion
- 2 garlic cloves
- 2 carrots
- 2 celery
- 6 brussels sprouts halved
- 1 zucchini

» Boil water with some salt and ½ onion and garlic.

» While you wait for the water to boil, mix the ground chicken/turkey, oats, tomatoes, onion, cilantro, egg and salt. Over the boiling water form little meatballs and drop them in the water.

» Once the meatballs have boiled with the water about 3 minutes and you see the majority of the meatballs floating, add all the vegetables and allow to boil one last time.

» You can add some organic chicken or vegetable stock for more flavor. Enjoy!

· Recipes | Main Dish ·

Chicken Soupy Rice

as dubbed by my son (this is a variation of the Nicaraguan dish known as Arroz Aguado and a great way to get kids to eat veggies)

by Krishna Sewal-Sandoval

Soup Ingredients: *This recipe will produce a thicker porridge-like consistency*

- 6-8 chicken drumsticks
- 2 Roma tomatoes
- 2 stalks of celery
- ¼ bunch of cilantro
- 1 large zucchini
- 3 lemons
- 1 tbsp of chicken bouillon
- 1 medium yellow onion
- 4 cloves of garlic
- 1 bunch of mint
- 2 yellow summer squashes
- Salt (to taste)
- 1 cup of Jasmine Rice
- About 8 cups of water

» Boil the chicken drumsticks in about 8 cups of water. Remove the foam once it has formed. If desired, you can remove the skin and shred the chicken off the bones (this will make it easier for little children to eat) Make sure to keep one of the bones in the soup to keep the flavor. Place the chicken back in the water.

» While the chicken is boiling, dice the onions and tomatoes. Mince the garlic, celery, mint and cilantro. Dice the zucchini and squash into bite sizes. Throw all the veggies into the water once the chicken has been shredded. Cook until squash and zucchini are soft. Once the veggies are soft, add salt to taste, chicken bouillon and squeeze the lemons into the soup.

» While the veggies continue cooking, fry the cup of Jasmine rice until it becomes opaque/golden. Once the veggies are soft, add the rice to the mixture. Continue cooking the soup until the rice splits. Wait until the soup cools and place in the fridge overnight so all of the flavor settles.

· Recipes | Main Dish ·

» Reheat on the stove and add about ½ cup of hot water with some bouillon so as not to dilute the flavor. Add pico de gallo if desired for a boost of flavor.

Pico de Gallo Ingredients: *Portions will vary based on individual's preference.*
- 5 tomatoes
- 1 bunch cilantro
- About 6 lemons
- 1½ large yellow onion
- 3 Thai chilis (optional)
- Salt (to taste)

» Squeeze the lemons into a bowl. Dice the tomatoes, onion and mince the cilantro and thai chilis — add to the lemon juice. Salt to taste. Pico de Gallo can sit overnight to allow the flavors to settle. Add to the soup or eat with the tostones.

Tostones Ingredients: *This is a Central American snack – a type of fried unripen banana chips. Make this the day you eat the soup as this does not reheat well*
- 4 plantains
- 4 cups of oil
- Salt (to taste)

» Peel the plantains and slice into about ¼ to ½ inch thickness. Once the oil is hot, add a few slices of the plantain chips at a time and fry until slightly golden. Once all of the chips have been fried, remove from the oil and mash each one. Add mashed chips back into the oil and continue frying until golden. It will continue to brown as it settles. As you remove the chips, transfer to a serving bowl and add salt so each chip has some salt. Eat immediately — you can top it off with pico de gallo.

· Recipes | Main Dish ·

Stuffed BBQ Chicken Breast
by Sydney Provost

Ingredients:
- 4 chicken breasts
- 1 tbsp olive oil
- 1 tsp paprika
- 1 tsp salt divided
- ¼ tsp BBQ seasoning
- ¼ tsp onion powder
- ¼ tsp chipotle seasoning
- 1½ cups chopped fresh spinach
- 4 oz. cream cheese, softened
- 1½ cups chopped mixed peppers
- 1 cup BBQ sauce your choice (Honey or hickory)
- ¼ cup grated cheese by choice (Preferably colby or cheddar)

» Preheat oven to 375 degrees.

» Add the ½ teaspoon salt, garlic powder, chipotle seasoning and onion powder to a small bowl and stir to combine. Sprinkle on both sides of chicken.

» Rub olive oil on chicken breasts. Cut a small opening in your chicken. Stuff chicken with your fillings (Cream cheese, spinach, grated cheese, bbq sauce and peppers).

» Bake for 20-30 minutes.

Best Crock-Pot Roast – Ever!
by Dona Flores

Ingredients:
- 1 chuck roast
- 1 jar peppercinis
- 1 cube butter

» Place chuck into crock pot. Put cube of butter on top of chuck. Cut stems off of peppercinis and put in crock pot. I use most of the jar and add juice from peppercinis (optional). Cook on low for 6 hours — you won't believe the flavors and how tender. OMG! Yum.

• Recipes | Desserts •

3 Minute Fudge
by Hope Carpenter

Ingredients:
- 3 cups (18 oz) chocolate chips,
  I used white chocolate chips, but any flavor will work
- 1 (14oz) can sweetened condensed milk
- 1/4 cup (4 tbsp) butter
- Optional: 1/2 tsp cinnamon, 1/4 tsp nutmeg, 1/4 tsp rum extract,
  1/2 cup chopped walnuts or pecans; sprinkles; cinnamon chips

Instructions:

» Spray an 8-inch square dish with cooking spray and set aside.

» Place chocolate chips, sweetened condensed milk, and butter in a large microwave-safe bowl. Heat in the microwave on high for 3-5 minutes, stirring every 30-60 seconds, just until the chocolate mixture is melted and completely combined.

» Stir in any mix-in's, such as cinnamon, nutmeg, rum extract, and sprinkles. Transfer chocolate mixture to prepared dish. Add sprinkles on top, if desired.

» Refrigerate until set and completely cool. Slice into squares and enjoy!

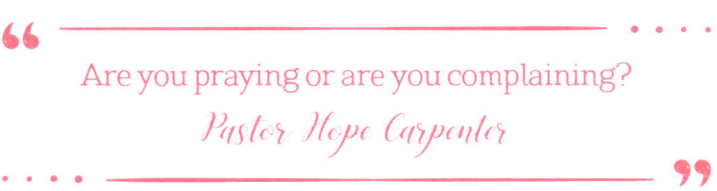

Are you praying or are you complaining?

Pastor Hope Carpenter

· Recipes | Desserts ·

Skillet Apple Pie
by Hope Carpenter

Ingredients:
- 2 lbs. Granny Smith apples
- 2 lbs. Braeburn apples
- ½ cup butter
- 1 cup firmly packed light brown sugar
- 1 (14.1-oz.) package refrigerated piecrusts
- 2 tbsp granulated sugar
- Butter-pecan ice cream
- 1 tsp ground cinnamon
- ¾ cup granulated sugar
- 1 egg white

How to Make It:

Step 1

Preheat oven to 350º. Peel apples, and cut into 1/2-inch-thick wedges. Toss apples with cinnamon and 3/4 cup granulated sugar.

Step 2

Melt butter in a 10-inch cast-iron skillet over medium heat; add brown sugar, and cook, stirring constantly, 1 to 2 minutes or until sugar is dissolved. Remove from heat, and place 1 piecrust in skillet over brown sugar mixture. Spoon apple mixture over piecrust, and top with remaining piecrust. Whisk egg white until foamy. Brush top of piecrust with egg white; sprinkle with 2 tbsp. granulated sugar. Cut 4 or 5 slits in top for steam to escape.

Step 3

Bake at 350º for 1 hour to 1 hour and 10 minutes or until golden brown and bubbly, shielding with aluminum foil during last 10 minutes to prevent excessive browning, if necessary. Cool on a wire rack 30 minutes before serving. Serve with butter-pecan ice cream.

· Recipes | Desserts ·

Carrot Cake
by Diane Hutchins

Cake Ingredients:

- 3 eggs
- 1¼ cups salad oil
- 2 tsp soda
- 2 tsp salt
- 2 tsp vanilla
- 2 cups sugar
- 2 cups flour
- 2 tsp cinnamon
- 2 cups grated carrots
- 1 cup coconut (for baking)
- 1¼ cups crushed pineapple (partially drained)
- 1 cup chopped nuts (I use walnuts)

Frosting Ingredients:

- 1 tsp vanilla
- 3 oz. cream cheese
- 2 or 3 tsp milk
- ½ cup butter (softened)
- 1 box powdered sugar

» Beat eggs then add sugar and oil and continue to beat. Sift dry ingredients and add until fully incorporated into egg/sugar/oil mixture. Stir in carrots and pineapple then stir in coconut and nuts. Add vanilla.

» Bake at 350° for 45-55 minutes in a 9x13 greased pan.

» For frosting, whip cream cheese and butter until creamy. Add sugar gradually and beat. Add vanilla. Sometimes 2 or 3 tsp milk are needed.

Recipes | Desserts

Esther's Special Carrot Cake
by Esther Garcia

Frosting Ingredients:
- 2 cups of sugar
- 1 cup of vegetable oil
- 2 oz of heavy whipping cream
- 4 eggs
- 2 tsp of vanilla extract

Carrot Cake Ingredients:
- 2 cups of sifted all purpose flour
- 1 tsp of baking powder
- 1 tsp of baking soda
- ½ teaspoon of salt
- 1 tsp of cinnamon
- 10 oz. of shredded carrots
- 1 cup of walnuts or 1 cup of mix unsalted nuts

» Mix frosting ingredients with a mixer, on medium speed, then put aside.

» Combine all the dry cake ingredients in a bowl, then combine with the wet cake ingredients a little at a time. Mix well on medium speed.

» Then blend in the shredded carrots and nuts.

» Bake at 350° for 24 to 30 minutes depending on what you use — cake pan or cupcake pan (cupcakes should be done at 24 minutes). Insert the carrot cake with a toothpick, if it comes out clean it is ready to remove from the oven.

» You can add some butter on top of the cake. Let it cool off, frost and enjoy!!!

· Recipes | Desserts ·

Easiest Cobbler EVER
by Hope Carpenter

- » Choose whatever canned fruit you like: peaches, cherries, etc.
- » Pour into casserole dish.
- » Cut pieces of bread into slices and lay over the fruit.
- » Melt stick of butter, or two depending on size of dish, and add cup of sugar.
- » Pour butter/sugar mixture over bread.
- » Bake at 375° until bubbly and bread is golden brown!!

Cracker Pie
by Diane Hutchins

Ingredients:
- 3 egg whites
- 1 cup sugar
- 1 tsp vanilla
- 14 soda crackers, coarsely crumbled
- ½ tsp cream of tartar
- ¾ cup chopped walnuts or pecans
- 1 cup heavy cream, whipped

- » Beat egg whites until foamy. Add cream of tartar and gradually add sugar and vanilla. Beat until stiff.
- » Fold in cracker crumbs and nuts. Spread in buttered 9-in pie pan. Bake at 300 degree oven for about 35 minutes. Cool at room temperature. When cold, spread with whipped cream and refrigerate at least 2 hours.
- » Slice into pie slices and serve.

· Recipes | Desserts ·

Sandy's Pumpkin Squares w/Cream Cheese Frosting
by Sandy Hutchins

Beat together:	– 4 large eggs	– 1 cup of oil
	– 1 16 oz. can of pumpkin	– 1⅔ cup of sugar
	– Optional: ½ tsp of ground ginger & ¼ tsp of ground cloves	
	Beat together until light & well mixed	
Then add:	– 2 cups of flour	– 2 tsp of cinnamon
	– 2 tsp of baking powder	– 1 tsp of soda
	– 1 tsp of salt	
	Mix well until no lumps & is light & fluffy	

» Preheat oven to 350°.

» Before you start, you can put your cream cheese & butter on the counter to soften in prep for your frosting.

» Use a jelly roll pan, it's like a cookie sheet with a 1-inch lip. Spray it with your favorite pan spray. Pour your batter into it & smooth it all out touching the sides.

» Bake 25-30 minutes. Always use a toothpick to check it and don't over bake it.

» When done, sit on a cooling rack to cool.

While pumpkin squares are cooling, we're going to make a cream cheese frosting.

Ingredients:
 – 1 8oz package of cream cheese-softened
 – ½ cup of butter-softened
 – 2 cups of powdered sugar
 – 1 teaspoon of vanilla

» Beat together cream cheese and butter until light and fluffy. Add sugar & vanilla & beat well. Spread onto cooled squares. Cut into 2" squares & enjoy.

Recipes | Desserts

Fried Cheerios
by Dona Flores

Ingredients:
- ½ stick of butter
- 6 cups of Honey Nut Cheerios

» Heat skillet or wok and melt the butter over medium to low heat.

» When the butter is all melted add the 6 cups of Honey Nut Cheerios and keep stirring until lightly brown.

» Add a little salt to taste or not and enjoy warm!

Peach Cobbler
by Tammy Mann

Ingredients:
- 1 cup flour
- 1 cup sugar
- 1 stick of butter
- 1 cup buttermilk or milk
- 1 can peaches drained

» Melt butter in oven safe dish 4×4 (clear dish preferred).

» Mix flour, sugar, milk or buttermilk in separate bowl and pour into butter. Do not stir. Drop in peaches.

» Bake at 350° for 35 to 40 minutes until golden brown.

» Recipe works also for apple cobbler.

· Recipes | Desserts ·

Caramel Pound Cake
by Mimi Addisu

Ingredients:
- 3 cups cake flour
- 3 cups brown sugar
- 1 tbsp vanilla
- ¼ teaspoon salt
- 1-8 oz. package cream cheese, room temperature
- 6 eggs, room temperature
- 3 sticks unsalted butter, room temperature

» Preheat oven to 300°.

» Spray a bundt pan with cooking spray and set aside.

» Cream butter and cream cheese in mixer for about 3-5 minutes. Add sugars slowly to butter/cream cheese mixture. Add eggs to mixture 1 at a time, beating for 20 seconds between the next egg. Add vanilla.

» Mix flour and salt together. Add in four batches to mixture. Scraping down sides of mixing bowl before adding last batch of flour.

» Pour mixture into baking pan. Tap baking pan on counter to remove air bubbles.

» Bake at 300 degrees for 1 hour and 30 minutes, check cake with a skewer for fork. Bake 10 minutes more if needed.

» Remove cake from oven, allow to cool 10 minutes in pan. Remove from pan and cool on cake platter for 30 more minutes.

· Recipes | Desserts ·

Caramel Sauce Ingredients:
- 1/4 cup water
- 1 cup granulated sugar
- ⅔ cup heavy whipping cream
- 3 tbsp unsalted butter, cut into tablespoon size pieces
- 1 tsp vanilla
- 1 tsp salt or to taste

» In a heavy bottomed saucepan, heat the water and sugar over medium heat. Make sure to use a saucepan that's a little bigger than what you think you will need. Stir constantly until the sugar has dissolved and the mixture starts to bubble just a little.

» Increase the heat to high and bring to a boil, stop stirring completely. Let the mixture continue boiling until it turns an amber color, this could take anywhere from 4-12 minutes.

» Remove from the heat and slowly whisk in the heavy cream. The mixture will bubble up quite a bit, so make sure to do this very carefully. Then, mix in the butter, vanilla, and salt one at a time.

» Pour the caramel sauce into a dish and allow to cool completely, then cover tightly and store in the refrigerator. The caramel sauce will thicken up some once it's cooled and refrigerated.

» Simply drizzle on pound cake or dare I say, ice cream!

· Recipes | Desserts ·

Sweet Potato Pie
by Julie Warren

My favorite pie was pumpkin and the idea of sweet potato pie sounded so weird and foreign! But my husband always raved that sweet potato pie was his favorite pie. So I went searching for a recipe and found this one. I'm lactose intolerant so I made a few substitutions to make it dairy-free. However, I'm including notes to make it with regular dairy as well. Both versions taste the same according to my husband.

Ingredients:
- 1 unbaked pie crust
- 1 cup sugar
- ¼ tsp baking soda
- 1.5 tsp pumpkin pie spice
- 2 beaten eggs
- ½ tsp salt
- 1 tsp vanilla extract
- 1 tbsp all purpose flour
- 2 cups cooked and mashed sweet potatoes
- 2 tbsp Smart Balance dairy-free margarine (or any dairy butter)
- ½ cup unsweetened almond milk
- 1-2 tsp apple cider vinegar (or ½ cup buttermilk)

» Preheat oven to 350°.

» Mix apple cider vinegar into almond milk and let rest at least five minutes.

» Mix together the sweet potato, margarine, and eggs. In a separate bowl mix together sugar, flour, salt, and pumpkin pie spice. Add dry ingredients to sweet potato mixture and stir well. Mix baking soda into almond milk (or buttermilk) and then add to sweet potato mixture, stir well. Mix in vanilla extract. Pour filling into pie crust.

» Bake in oven for 60-70 minutes, or until set in the center. Cool, slice, and serve!

· Recipes | Desserts ·

Chocolate Chunk Oatmeal Cookies
by Lupe Soto

Ingredients:
- 6 tbsp unsalted butter
- ⅓ cup all-purpose flour
- ¾ tsp baking soda
- ½ tsp salt
- 1 tsp vanilla extract
- ¾ cup light brown sugar
- ⅓ cup whole wheat flour
- 1½ cups old fashion oats
- 1 egg
- ½ cup chopped walnuts
- 3 oz. bittersweet chocolate coarsely chopped

» Pre-heat oven to 350

» Melt 6 tbs unsalted butter in a small sauce pan over low heat. Remove from heat and add ¾ cup light brown sugar, stir until smooth.

» Combine ⅓ cup all-purpose flour, ⅓ cup whole wheat flour, ¾ tsp baking soda and 1½ cups old fashion oats, and ½ tsp salt, in a medium bowl.

» Combine butter mixture with the dry ingredients and add 1 egg lightly beaten. Add 1 tsp vanilla extract. Fold in ½ cup chopped walnuts and 3 oz. bittersweet chocolate coarsely chopped. Mix well and spoon by tablespoon onto a lightly greased baking sheet.

» Bake for 12 min

» Makes 32 cookies. Cookies freeze well… they are very yummy, Enjoy!

· Recipes | Desserts ·

S'mores Chocolate Chip Cookies
by Denise Lopez

Ingredients:
- 2⅓ cups all-purpose flour
- 1 tsp baking soda
- ½ tsp salt
- 2 sticks (8 oz.) unsalted butter
- 1 cup light brown sugar
- ½ cup granulated sugar
- 2 tsp vanilla
- 2 large eggs
- 1 cup mini marshmallows
- 2 cups semi-sweet chocolate chips
- ½ cup graham cracker crumbs, finely crushed

» Preheat oven to 375°. Line 2 large baking sheets with parchment paper and set aside. In a medium-sized bowl whisk together the flour, graham cracker crumbs, baking soda, and salt; set aside.

» In the bowl of a standing mixer fitted with the paddle attachment, add the butter and both sugars; beat on medium-speed for 2 to 3 minutes, or until light and fluffy. Add the vanilla and beat smooth. Beat in the eggs, one at a time, beating well after each addition. Reduce mixer speed to low and gradually add in the flour mixture. Be sure not to over beat here! Using a sturdy spatula or wooden spoon, fold in chocolate chips, marshmallows, and graham crackers.

» Roll 3 tablespoon sized portions of dough between your palms to form a ball (they should be big; almost a ¼ cup), then place on prepared sheet (make sure to leave 2" between each cookie for inevitable spreading). Continue this process until all the dough has been rolled. Place baking sheets in preheated oven, one at a time, and bake for 11 to 12 minutes, or until golden at the edges but still soft in the middle. Let cookies cool for 10 minutes on the sheet before transferring to a wire rack to cool completely.

· Recipes | Desserts ·

Pookie's Cookies – Caramel Oatmeal Cookies
by Denise Lopez

10 minute prep time. 10 minute cook time.

Ingredients:
- 1 ½ cups all purpose flour
- 1 tsp cinnamon
- 2 eggs
- 1 cup (2 sticks) butter, softened
- ¾ cup granulated sugar
- ¾ cup packed light brown sugar
- 3 cups quick or old-fashion oats, uncooked
- 1 package Ghirardelli caramel chips
- 1 tsp baking soda
- 1 tsp salt
- 1 tsp vanilla extract

» Preheat oven to 350°.

» In a small bowl, combine flour, baking soda, cinnamon and salt.

» In a large bowl, cream together butter, granulated sugar, brown sugar, eggs and vanilla extract. Gradually beat in flour mixture. Fold in oats and caramel bits.

» Drop by rounded Tablespoons onto baking sheets lined with parchment paper.

» Cook for 10-12 minutes, or until golden brown.

Also wanted to mention that I enjoy baking. My grandma (Nana) was a second mom to me. She enjoyed baking as well. So when I bake, I'm reminded of her. When I bake, I also enjoy listening to music and sometimes will dance while I bake. Dancing adds extra sass to my baking.

· Recipes | Desserts ·

Chocolate Covered Cranberry Walnut Cookies
by Sandy Hutchins

Mix together:
- 1 cup of butter-softened
- ¾ cup of sugar
- ¾ cup of brown sugar
- 1 teaspoon of vanilla
- 2 eggs

Slowly add to mixture:
- 2¼ cups of flour
- 1 teaspoon of baking soda
- 1 teaspoon of salt
- 1 cup of dried cranberries
- 1 cup of chopped walnuts

Note: a few lumps are ok to leave in the mixture

» I use a small cookie scooper to form balls of dough & drop them onto your greased cookie sheet. The dough will spread out so make sure you space them. Bake at 350° for about 10-12 minutes. Everyone's oven will vary. I like them a little brown around the edges.

» While they're cooking, put paper towels onto your counter and lay them on to cool. Make sure they're not touching.

» While your cookies are cooling, melt 1 cup of chocolate chips (semi or milk). When they are cooled, drizzle the chocolate over each one. You can make your own designs if you like or just use lines of chocolate across each cookie. Enjoy. They will melt in your mouth.

· Recipes | Desserts ·

1-1-1 Cookie
by Gina Libbee

Kid pleaser of all ages, guaranteed! When you or the kids want something sweet and there's nothing handy, or you don't have the time for some outlandish recipe nor do you have any boxed cake in the cupboards. Well I have the best and simplest recipe for you. You don't even need a pen or paper.

Ingredients:
- 1 cup of butter
- 1 cup of peanut butter
- 1 egg

» Preheat oven 350°.

» In large bowl, mix 1 cup of sugar, 1 cup of peanut butter (crunchy or smooth it doesn't matter) and 1egg.

» Roll it until it looks like you're ready to bake cookie dough from the market. Put dough in ziploc bag sprayed with non-stick cooking spray and then place in the freezer for 7 minutes.

» While that's in the freezer you spray non-stick cooking spray on a cookie sheet. After the 7 minutes is over, take cookie dough out of the freezer. Cut dough into ¼-inch slices place on cookie sheet then take a fork and press criss-cross marks in the cookie. You can add white/dark chocolate chips or nuts in the dough.

» Put in oven and bake for 8 to 10 minutes. Take out the oven let it cool off for 4 to 5 minutes. It's the best and the healthiest peanut butter cookie you'll ever taste.

· Recipes | Cooking Measurements ·

U.S. to METRIC

CAPACITY

1/5 teaspoon	1 milliliter
1 teaspoon	5 ml
1 tablespoon	15 ml
1 fluid oz	30 ml
1/5 cup	47 ml
1 cup	237 ml
2 cups (1 pint)	473 ml
4 cups (1 quart)	.95 liter
4 quarts (1 gallon)	3.8 liters

WEIGHT

1 oz.	28 grams
1 pound	454 grams

· Recipes | Cooking Measurements ·

1 tablespoon (tbsp) = 3 teaspoons (tsp)
1/16 cup = 1 tablespoon
1/8 cup = 2 tablespoons
1/6 cup = 2 tablespoons + 2 teaspoons
1/4 cup = 4 tablespoons
1/3 cup = 5 tablespoons + 1 teaspoon
3/8 cup = 6 tablespoons
1/2 cup = 8 tablespoons
2/3 cup = 10 tablespoons = 2 teaspoons
3/4 cup = 12 tablespoons
1 cup = 48 teaspoons
1 cup = 16 tablespoons
8 fluid ounces (fl oz) = 1 cup
1 pint (pt) = 2 cups
1 quart (qt) = 2 pints
4 cups = 1 quart
1 gallon (gal) = 4 quarts
16 ounces (oz) = 1 pound (lb)
1 milliliter (ml) = 1 cubic centimeter (cc)
1 inch (in) = 2.54 centimeters (cm)

> God doesn't reward the dreamer. He rewards the diligent seeker.
> *Pastor Hope Carpenter*

table manners

> Good manners have much to do with the emotions. To make them ring true, one must feel them, not merely exibit them.

Amy Vanderbilt

· Table Manners ·

how to SET a TABLE
For any formal or informal occasion

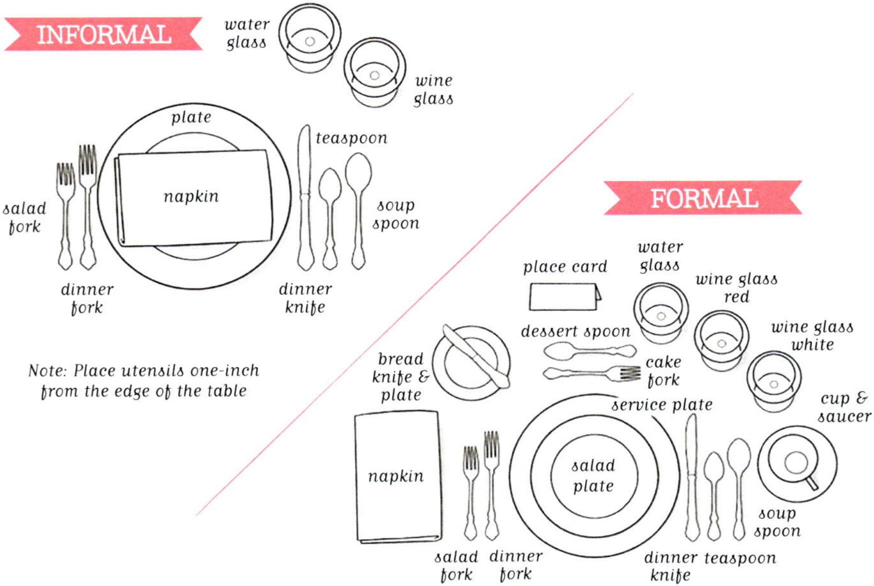

INFORMAL

FORMAT

Note: Place utensils one-inch from the edge of the table

Note: The cup & saucer are to be placed on the table during the dessert course.

Table Manners

It might have been a while since your parents drummed correct table manners into you, so a quick refresher course is not a bad thing. Remember, this is less about adhering to some archaic set of rules and more about showing respect to those around you. Let your conversation and sparkling company shine through, unimpeded by rude and distracting behavior. Here are the golden rules:

The Golden Rules of Table Decorum

» Start with good posture: Don't slouch over your food. Sit up straight in your chair and do not rest your elbows on the table.

» Don't fidget, play with your napkin, or peel candle wax off the tablecloth.

» Wait until everyone is seated before starting your food.

» Don't season your food until you've tried it.

» Eat by bringing your fork or spoon up to your mouth, rather than lowering your mouth down to your plate.

» Ask for food to be passed to you rather than reaching over people.

» Do not rest your knife and fork in between bites so you don't rush your food.

» Try not to leave food on your plate, as this could offend your host.

How to Use a Napkin

Step One:	Lay a napkin over your lap; never tuck it into your shirt!
Step Two:	Bring it up to your lips to dab them lightly rather than rubbing them.
Step Three:	If you leave the table during a meal, leave your napkin on your seat until you return
Step Four:	Once you have finished eating, put your napkin on the table, to the side of your dirty plate — never on top.

How to Handle Your Cutlery

- Navigate your cutlery by starting with the ones on the outside and working your way in. If in doubt, wait for others to pick theirs up first and follow their lead.
- If only a fork is provided (with risotto, for example), use it in your right hand with the prongs facing upward, like a spoon; otherwise, use it in your left hand, prongs facing downward, with a knife.
- After you've finished eating, lay your knife and fork side by side in the middle of your plate with the handles pointed toward you and with the prongs of the fork pointing upward.
- Never put your knife in your mouth!

· Table Manners ·

International Business Etiquette

Think about traveling for business as a form of international diplomacy. To be just as ladylike abroad as you are at home, you need to be educated about the country's culture and customs. Women are perceived very differently in different continents and learning to embrace these differences will help you to be more accepted.

As a general rule, follow the lead of your hosts. Keep an open mind when it comes to dining—while you can politely decline those monkey brains, sampling them could secure you the deal and might well be worth it. Study the most important customs of the country before you visit. In the meantime, here are some key pointers:

Asia

- » Avoid showing too much skin, as revealing clothes are unacceptable. Jeans are fine for evenings, but not for meetings.
- » Personal contact must be avoided at all cost. It is highly inappropriate for a man to touch a woman in public
- » Always arrive on time or early if you are the guest.
- » Bowing or nodding is a more usual greeting than a handshake.
- » All greetings should be formal, so use a full name in an introduction.
- » Do not discuss everything on your plate, as this implies you have not been given enough and you are still hungry

International Business Etiquette

Latin America

- » While sexy styles of dress may be beach-worthy, stick to dark suits and white shirts for business meetings.
- » Always maintain eye contact.
- » Eating on the street or on public transport is considered extremely rude.
- » Titles are very important — always address a person by their professional title only, such as "professor" for teacher or "abogado" for lawyer (in Spanish-speaking countries).
- » Good relationships will help shorten what can otherwise become lengthy negotiations. Work hard to build a relationship before you even start doing business.
- » Be punctual but expect to wait up to 30 minutes for your counterpart.
- » Touching each other's arms or pats on the back are recognized signs of friendship

· Table Manners ·

International Business Etiquette

Middle East

- » Women must keep their upper arms, chest, back, and legs covered at all times, and wear long pants while exercising.
- » Try not to use the word "no," which can offend. Evasive refusals are more appropriate. Never refuse an invitation outright; instead, refer to a clash of engagements.
- » Do not thank your host at the end of a meal, as this is considered a form of payment and is therefore insulting.
- » It is common to remove your shoes before entering a building — follow the lead of your host.
- » Bare in mind that alcohol and pork are illegal in Saudi Arabia.
- » Friday is the day of rest for Muslims so do not arrange a business meeting on this day.
- » The left hand is considered unclean, so do not shake hands or eat with it.
- » Try not to cross your legs when sitting and never show the bottom of your feet, as these are considered disrespectful.
- » The thumbs-up gesture is offensive. Use it at your peril.

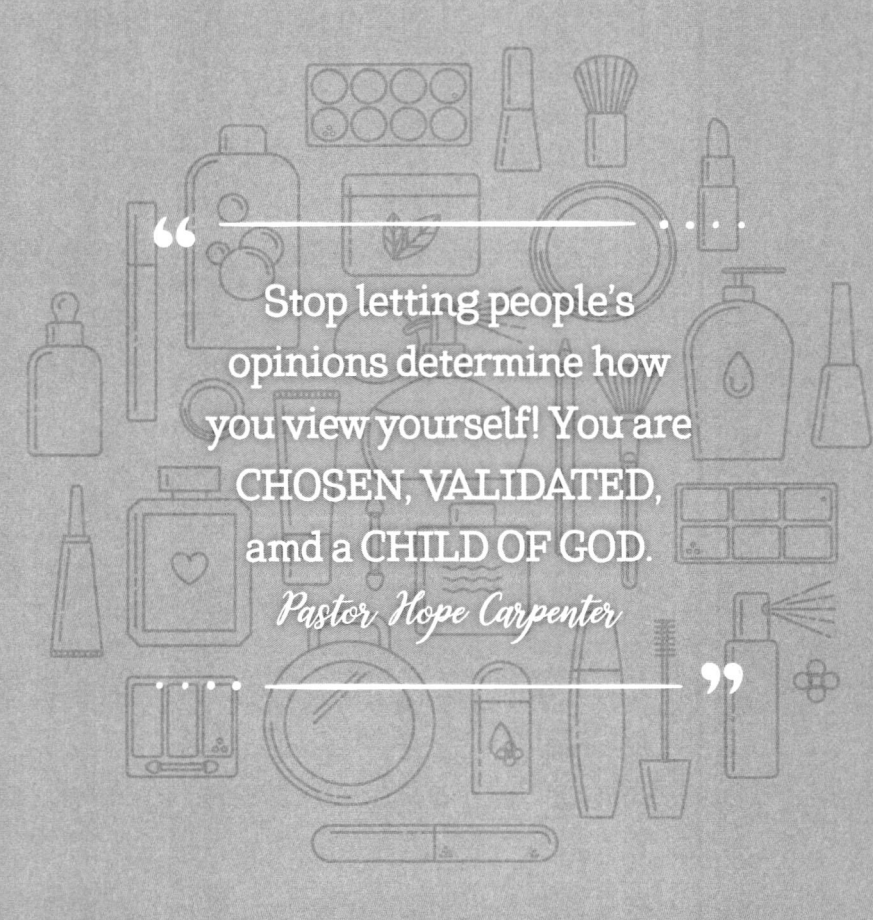

beauty tips

> "You will be adorned with beauty and grace, and wisdom's glory will wrap itself around you, making you victorious in the race."

Proverbs 4:9

· Beauty Tips ·

To keep your makeup from transferring, after you apply your foundation/concealer, spray your entire face with water and take a wet make-up sponge and dab the water into your skin. Then, set your makeup with a powder.

∾ Lexi Solis ∾

For an "au natural" look that takes less than 5 minutes try a little bit of concealer... it goes a long way. Put only on areas that are red, dark or could benefit from a little touch up. Top with a dewy rose blush, a little mascara and a tinted lip balm and your good to go.

∾ Chinere Mcdaniels ∾

Use baby oil to remove makeup instead of expensive products.

∾ "T" Watson ∾

To fast dry polished nails use a hand blow dryer, it's faster than waiting to air dry and it ensures you get completely dried nails. Works great when in a hurry and have to go out.

∾ Shirley Starghill ∾

· Beauty Tips ·

Natural Beauty scrub

- 1/2 cup of brown sugar
- 2 tbsp of honey
- 1 tbsp of lemon juice
- 1 tbsp of scented oil of choice (optional)

This scrub can be used on your lips, hands and feet, when scrubbed on your skin, leaving it silky soft and smelling amazing! This natural beauty scrub also works well as a gift for a loved one.

∾ Dulce Farfan Ruiz ∾

To improve my hair from being dry and dull, I use coconut oil twice a week. I massage my scalp and leave on the coconut oil overnight and hair feels softer and shinier and it also helps prevent falling hair too.

∾ Ning De Guzman ∾

Collagen powder in my Nutri bullet shakes changed my skin and makes this 40 year old look 25 all day. Everyday!

∾ Erica Rangel ∾

· *Beauty Tips* ·

Tips for wearing make-up during the summer. Get a good setting spray to set your make-up and to keep your face makeup looking fresh!

≈ *Maricela Valencia* ≈

Make up tip: Prevent clumps in your mascara by running it under hot water.

Coffee Face Mask
For smooth and clear skin use coffee grounds and milk.
For firm and tight skin use yogurt, coffee grounds and honey.

≈ *Amanda Perez* ≈

Eye tightener » Take one egg and separate the yolk from the egg white. Use egg white only; store in tupperware and refrigerate for daily use. Put dabs of egg white underneath and around your eyes, let it dry and let the tightness begin. After 30 min wash/rinse with water, then moisturize!

≈ *Jeannette Reynoso-Anderson* ≈

A little drop of lotion will take the frizz out of your hair if your on the go.

≈ *Khaliah Calderon* ≈

· Beauty Tips ·

Always rinse your face after washing with cold water to close and shrink your pores for the day. You can even put your toner in an ice tray with a toothpick in it and apply it to your face after washing. This method of rinsing and toning lessens the manifestation of pimples, blackheads, whiteheads and gives the face a more matte and smoother appearance.

———————

Also, anyone can wear just about any color of lipstick or lip-gloss regardless of your skin tone and lip fullness if you line your lips with a darker than lipstick or lip-gloss color lip liner.

———————

Bonus Beauty tips: Rinsing a face with milk will aide in evening out your skin tone and adding tightness to the skin.

———————

An oatmeal (oatmeal and purified water sitting in a bowl for about 20 mins before applying) mask is great for skin elasticity, tone, and oil control.

———————

Turmeric, yogurt and honey is a great face mask or body mask for anti-aging, brightening, getting rid of age spots and free-radicals and adding antioxidants.

———————

Avocado, egg, and olive oil is a miracle hair mask/conditioner for color damaged, heat damaged, dry, brittle and breaking hair. Blend 1 whole avocado, 1 egg, and 1/3 cup olive oil. Place mixture on hair, use a plastic cap and a towel around your neck for any dripping. Leave on for a minimum of 1 hour. For a complete overhaul leave in overnight, but cover your pillow. Afterwards rinse, wash and towel dry as normal.

≈ *Jessica Young* ≈

• Beauty Tips •

To dry your freshly painted nails faster, spray Pam (cooking spray) on top.

~ Melissa Hayashida ~

Sites to get free full-size beauty products and or coupons to pick them up in store.

influenster.com
pinchme.com
mysavings.com
closetfreesamples.com

~ Sharonda Williams ~

Face Mask: 1 egg yolk, ¼ teaspoon turmeric, 1 teaspoon olive oil.

Directions: Mix ingredients together until it becomes a paste, apply to face, let it dry for about 10-20 min or till paste has completely dried on face. Rinse off once finished, and apply favorite moisturizer.

~ Archal Swamy ~

When you remove your makeup, wash your eyelids in baby shampoo to avoid eye infection. It works.

~ Gloria Holmes ~

· Beauty Tips ·

As a former beauty consultant, we always told our clients not to pump their mascara because it introduces a lot of air that drys out your mascara. A solution to the dry tube of mascara is to put the tube in a cup of hot water (180 degrees at least) while you are putting the rest of your make up on. Give it about 10 minutes and then use. You will find that your mascara is no longer dry. You can do this for a while until you buy another tube.

∼ Marilyn Tinsley ∼

For Soft Skin (specifically feet), put Vaseline or Bag Balm (Vermont's Original Skin) on your feet & put socks on before bed. Wake up to super soft feet!

∼ Sandra Pina ∼

Tip on how to open that nail polish bottle that you can't open no matter how hard you try. Fill a microwave safe cup or bowl with water. Fill it enough to completely submerge the nail polish. Heat water for about 1.5 to 2 minutes. Place the bottle of nail polish in the hot water and soak for about 5-10 minutes. Remove the bottle from the water and open!

∼ Chantal Dumont ∼

Best natural products for curly hair Is Cantu. Wet your hair completely, brush thoroughly and add some Cantu curl cream, next add some Cantu mega hold styling stay glue gel. Works amazing ! Everyone always asks what products I use. You can find these products at any Sally beauty store or Walmart.

∼ Kayla Powdar ∼

· Beauty Tips ·

Essential Oils!!!! I have always had terrible skin issues, from eczema to acne and excess oil. My skin is sensitive and most products make me itch or breakout. Until the day I was introduced to essential oils, more specifically Young Living Essential Oils. (I am not a sales person for this company, just a girl wanting to empower other woman in all aspects of their life).

They are pure, organic, and they have multiple uses. I started using lavender, frankincense, and Rose oil blended in almond oil or coconut oil on my skin and saw an immediate difference in the tone, fine lines, age spots, and blemishes. Things healed faster, didn't leave behind dark spots or scars, and my skin glowed! And I had less breakouts.

Those expensive over the counter and prescription acne and facial washes and creams are harsh and full of chemicals that can actually have serious side effects. Try the oils!!! Your skin will love you for it! You will have a multipurpose, aromatic, arsenal of products that can help with anything from stains, bug repellent, air purifier, muscle aches, headaches, stomach issues, immune support and even teething, grumpy babies and toddlers.

Oils can offer emotional and spiritual support. Even God's word mentions the oils and their medicinal power!!! I could honestly go on and on and on about the health and beauty benefits and solutions that essential oils offer. Go try them for yourselves and spread the word to all the ladies you love.

~ *Sara Toney* ~

· Beauty Tips ·

For Women who have African braids and find that they are way too tight, here's a great tip: Take a small spray bottle and fill it with ice water and spray it directly on your scalp immediately after it's been braided and it gives instant relief.

≈ *Paula Ferguson* ≈

My biggest advice would be to hide those greys. Very few can pull off grey unless your 85 maybe. I know a few gorgeous natural silver- and white-haired ladies. It depends on skin tone and style. Your haircut should frame and flatter your beautiful face. If you have had the same haircut for years … CHANGE IT! Try something new. Soft highlights to bold colors. It is our crowning glory!

BEAUTY is also within, you must love yourself and be proud of who you are. We are God's glorious daughters. You have to be a whole loving person to be who He wants you to be! God bless you my dear friends!

≈ *Cynthia Lara* ≈

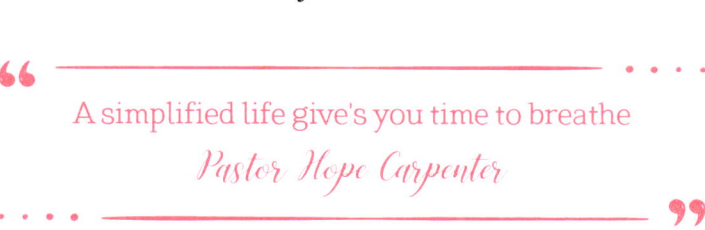

" A simplified life give's you time to breathe
Pastor Hope Carpenter "

· Beauty Tips ·

Eyelash Extension Cleanser Recipe

- 2 tbsp baby shampoo
- 12 tbsp bottled/distilled water
- Mix well in foam pump bottle

Wash eyelash extensions with makeup brush or fingers. Rinse well. Blow dry lashes on cool setting. Blot dry with towel. Brush them out to fluff them beauties out to salute the world.

~ *Adrienne Spencer* ~

Easy Face Mask. Scramble 1 egg, apply it to your face and neck — except keep out of your eyes. Let it dry (don't smile) and then wash it with warm water and then rinse with cold water and pat dry. You can do this 3 times a week.

~ *Carla Johnson* ~

Trying to get a great beach wave lived in look, try putting come curls in your hair before bed with a curling iron and using some sea salt texture spray. The next morning you'll have great texture and the perfect just enough wave for the day! I tell my clients this all the time!! Best products for curls and waves: sea salt texture spray & texture powder.

~ *Darcy Fernandez* ~

· Beauty Tips ·

These beauty tips work for everyone …
short or tall, young or old, thin or fat, every race and color!

- For attractive lips, speak words of kindness.
- For lovely eyes, seek out the good in people.
- For a slim figure, share your food with the hungry.
- For beautiful hair, let a child run his or her fingers through it once a day.
- For poise, walk with the knowledge that you never walk alone. People, even more than things, have to be restored, renewed, revived, reclaimed and redeemed; never throw out anyone.
- Remember if you ever need a helping hand, you'll find one at the end of each of your arms. As you grow older, you will discover that you have two hands; one for helping yourself, the other for helping others.
- The beauty of a woman is not in the clothes she wears, the figure that she carries, or the way she combs her hair.
- The beauty of a woman must be seen from in her eyes, because that is the doorway to her heart, the place where love resides.
- The beauty of a woman is not in a facial mole, but the true beauty in a woman is reflected in her soul.
- It is the caring that she lovingly gives, the passion that she shows.
- The beauty of a woman grows with the passing years.

Author: Audrey Hepburn, when asked to share her beauty tips.

~ *Diana Dorn* ~

• Beauty Tips •

Women's Clothing Sizes

US	UK	Japan	France, Spain & Portugal	Germany & Scandinavia	Italy	Australia & New Zealand
6	6/8	7-9	36	34	40	8
8	10	9-11	38	36	42	10
10	12	11-13	40	38	44	12
12	14	13-15	42	39	46	14
14	16	15-17	44	40	48	16
16	18	17-19	46	42	50	18
18	20	19-21	48	44	52	20

> Jesus loves you –
> cellulite and all.
> *Pastor Hope Carpenter*

· Beauty Tips ·

Women's Shoe Sizes

US	European	UK	Japanese
5	35.5	3	22.5
5 ½	36	3 ½	23
6	37	4	23
6 ½	37.5	4 ½	23.5
7	38	5	24
7 ½	39	5 ½	24
8	39.5	6	24.5
8 ½	40	6 ½	25
9 ½	41	7	25.5
10	41.5	7 ½	26
10 ½	42	8	26.5

> If the shoe fits — buy it in every color!
> *Pastor Hope Carpenter*

body talk

> "Or do you not know that your body is a temple of the Holy Spirit within you, whom you have from God? You are not your own, for you were bought with a price. So glorify God in your body."
>
> 1 Corinthians 6:19-20

Body Talk

Positive Body Language

- » Eye contact.
- » Open palms.
- » Legs crossed at the ankle.
- » Smiling and nodding.
- » Standing up straight.
- » Facing toward the person you're speaking to.
- » Sitting upright.

Negative Body Language

- » Hunched shoulders.
- » Folded arms.
- » No eye contact.
- » Turning away from the person you're speaking to.
- » Legs crossed at the knee.
- » Slouching in your seat
- » Frowning

> "If you try to have your hands on everything, you won't influence anything."
>
> *Pastor Hope Carpenter*

health and fitness

> Beloved, I pray you to prosper concerning all things and to be in good health, just as your soul prospers.

3 John 1:2

· Health & Fitness ·

Tummy Problems

Get ginger root and add to water and drink as hot tea or just in glass of water.

Detox Water

Water, sliced cucumbers, ginger root, lemons and pineapples. Drink all day.

∽ *Hope Carpenter* ∽

Keep Legs Loooong and Leeean

Jump rope 5 minutes a day. Count 120 jumps for 1 minute worth and then repeat 4 more times. The correct way to jump (by skipping) will develop balance, tone the core, quads, hams, and calves.

Dont forget to stretch legs!

∽ *Sandra Gomez* ∽

Sinus Infection

Slice a fresh lemon and put 3 drops of lemon juice on a spoon and inhale the drops in each nostril. This will help with the sinus infection. 2 times a day will help stop the infection. Lemon is an antibacterial.

∽ *Joahne Francis* ∽

· Health & Fitness ·

Tension Headaches

Use peppermint oil in the back of the skull (Occipital Ridge) to decrease tension headaches. And take 3 deep conscious breathes.

≈ *"T" Watson* ≈

Quick Workout

Use "Quick Fit" app. It is a 7 minute quick workout that can be done anywhere. I use at work on breaks!

≈ *Lissa Cato* ≈

Skin Care

Hey Girls! If I wasn't a wedding photographer then I'd be a skin advocate! I have girls 15 years younger than me ask me all the time what do I use on my skin. I turned 42 this year but most think I am 25+. Living surrendered to Jesus definitely keeps you looking youthful but in addition is SUNBLOCK. Not just any sunblock but sunblock with zinc. If your sunblock does not have zinc then it is not blocking the damaging rays that cause aging. Even when working from home I wear sunblock. If you are ever exposed to the light then you need to protect your skin.

You can def find one that is not too thick or heavy. I prefer SkinCeuticals Ultimate UV Defense SPF 30. It's not cheap but it's so worth it. Cheers to your health!

≈ *Leah Carson* ≈

· Health & Fitness ·

Keep Hydrated

I find that dehydration is a major cause of sickness, and many times we don't even realize we're simply thirsty! A few tips I have making sure we drink plenty of water are:

1. Buy your favorite, filtered water. You're more likely to drink up if you've paid a bit.
2. Drink a glass of fresh lemon water first thing in the morning when you wake up. It's a nice wake-up drink and settles your stomach.
3. Strive to drink at least half your body weight in fluid ounces.
4. Download an app to remind you to drink water. I downloaded the Daily Water app and set it to remind me every two hours.
5. Flavor it up with fresh fruit. Cucumber water is delicious!
6. Carry a water bottle with you wherever you go so it's always with you and you're constantly reminded to drink up!

I hope these tips have been helpful! You can find more at:
www.christianhomeschoolmoms.com

~ ***Demetria Zinga*** ~

Fever Remedy

Infants, babies, and Big Babies - If your running a fever an old remedy is to rub rubbing alcohol on the soles of the feet to let the heat out of the body. You don't need much and can repeat every hour.

~ ***Carla Johnson*** ~

· Health & Fitness ·

No Diet plan

Do a calorie count plan. Count your calories daily! Figure out your height and true weight to know how many calories you should intake daily. This will help maintain your weight always. (And a detox tea can always help)

∼ *Rachel Arias* ∼

Tea Time

I have found drinking herbal tea is a great way to help with keeping my body healthy. My latest find is Roobis Tea. It taste scrumptious with a Splenda packet (or sugar of your choice) added. I find it helps with curving my appetite when I add a teaspoon of Chia to my cup of tea. The brand I choose is Celestial, I found at my local grocery store. Through this discovery, I have added lemon & ginger along with Raspberry flavors and there are many more herbal flavors to choose in this catagory.

∼ *Carrie Gordon* ∼

Quick Weightloss

The quickest way to lose weight: high intensity intervals. 60 seconds of jumping jacks, high knee running whatever ... just get your heart rate as high as you can. Then 60 seconds ... just marching in place (focus on relaxing your heart rate) then do it again. Doing 8 sets total on alternating days. Takes only about 20 minutes but it gives results! You can even do 30 seconds on and 30 seconds slow.

Food goals: eat 10 servings of fruits and vegetables a day. You'll be so full you won't have room for junk! If you stick to this you can even have a cheat meal once a week!

∼ *Olympia Peralta* ∼

· Health & Fitness ·

Inspiration

I would like to inspire women to take care of ourselves. We often give so freely, take infrequently causing us to lose ourselves. In this moment remember selfcare is just as important as any other thing that is happening in our lives. Therefore, I encourage you to love you, and remember everything will be alright. "All things works together for good for them who love the Lord." – Romans 8:28.

≈ ***Yula Victoria*** ≈

Detox Recipe

Hello! I would like to give a healthy tip that everyone can benefit from. I recently decided to detox my body from toxins and to feel more energized. I cut up 1 lemon, 1 cucumber, and threw in pure mint leaves into a jug of water. I let it sit for at least 2 hours and drink anywhere from 5-8 cups a day. It's great, trust me!

≈ ***Chavarra Stanley*** ≈

Healthy & Safe Mommy Tip

Most mom's I know have a handy emergency kit for cuts and bruises. I like to keep a RED WASHCLOTH in my kit. Why? Little kiddos panic when they see blood (sometimes even mommy does too), so using a red washcloth cuts down on the panic and helps keep them calm while we take care of the emergency. It is thick enough to absorb and helps add pressure.

≈ ***Shawn Renee Robinson*** ≈

· Health & Fitness ·

Apple Cider Vinegar

1 tbsp of apple cider vinegar in a glass of water will do the following:

- » Clear up heartburn almost instantly.
- » Destroy stomach viruses (diarrhea).
- » Cuts time with the flu in half, stops it completely if you catch it in time.
- » Aids digestion (especially if you don't have a gallbladder).
- » Helps lose fat (good for dieting).
- » Helps clear the mind/memory from foggyness from unhealthy eating (brain power)
- » Good internally for clearing the skin. Topically as a toner to clear up breakouts and keep away blackheads. Keeps skin healthy.
- » Put ACV on burns (including sunburns) to stop "cooking" and release heat from under skin (doesn't sting). I put mustard on burns as well for my clumsy kitchen burns (not water), vinegar is in mustard.

~ *Gabriella Quintero* ~

Cure for Mosquito Bites

If you get a mosquito bite or a bug bite and want the redness and toxins from spreading, put a bentonite clay mask over the bite and leave it on for 30 minutes.

You can use bentonite powder mixed with water to create the mask or you can buy a ready-made mask. Use brand Redmond facial mud, it works every time for me and my kids.

~ *Rowena Quianzon* ~

> "God needs your talent, gifts, and your submission for His will to be done."
>
> *Pastor Hope Carpenter*

diy projects

> May the favor of the Lord our God rest on us;
> establish the work of our hands for us —
> yes, establish the work of our hands.

Psalm 90:17

• *DIY Projects* •

Solution for Oil Stains

Ladies have you ever spilled something oil based or been cooking and had gravy or sauce splatter on your blouse or dress? Well here are 4 easy steps to get an oil based stain out of your clothing.

- » Shake an ample amount of baby powder on any oil-based stain.
- » Let it sit for at least 24 hours.
- » Dust off excess powder. Spot treat stain with a grease fighting dish soap.
- » Rinse thoroughly and hang dry.

Repeat steps for stubborn stains.

~ Camille Crawford ~

Bible DIY for Kids

Help kids make bible teachings relatable with this fun project. Have the child trace their hands on construction paper and label it "My Prayer Book." They can then put scriptures in the book along with how the scripture can be used every day.

~ Jesse Harden ~

Portable Bible Verses

On index cards, write down Bible verses that you or your children are learning then punch a hole in the corner and put them on a metal ring. You can keep them in your purse or backpack and bring them wherever you go.

~ Hope Carpenter ~

· DIY Projects ·

On-The-Go Baby Snacks Storage

While traveling with a baby that eats puffs, use an empty water bottle. The packaging it comes in opens and spills easily and an empty water bottle assures it stays closed.

Getting Rid of Bad Smells

Pour 1 cup of white vinegar in the wash to get rid of the bad smell in clothes.

Baby Cuddle Trick

If you co-sleep with your baby or want your baby to have the cuddle feeling in their crib, roll 2 towels and shape them in a circle under the sheets.

~ *Melissa Hayashida* ~

- -

Get Rid of Water Rings on Wood Furniture

To get water rings out of furniture take a half teaspoon of olive oil and a half teaspoon of white vinegar, mix together on a cloth and rub with the grain of the wood and voilà!!!

~ *Pam Smith* ~

> *God loved you when your past was still your future.*
>
> *Pastor Hope Carpenter*

· DIY Projects ·

How to Remove Soap Scum & Film From Your Shower Doors for Good

Have you ever scrubbed down your shower doors only to find them streaky and covered with film an hour later? I have a simple solution that my grandmother taught me as a child which doesn't require a lot of time or work to get your shower doors sparkly clean and prevent them from getting covered in film again.

You'll need:
- An old white rag, cloth or paper towel (must be white and free of color).
- Baby oil or mineral oil.

Instructions:
1. Make sure your shower doors are completely dry.
2. Squeeze baby or mineral oil on your cloth (a little goes a long way).
3. Starting from the top of your shower doors, wipe in an S pattern and work your way down.
4. Apply more oil to your cloth as needed until you're done.

And that's it! The oil breaks down dirt and soap film on your shower doors, making it easy to remove with a cloth or paper towel. It also creates a barrier on the wall which helps to prevent soap and dirt from sticking to it in the future.

~ *Dela Antoinette* ~

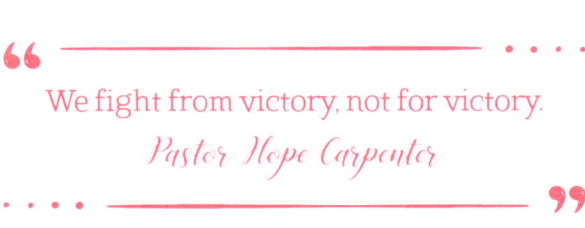

> We fight from victory, not for victory.
>
> *Pastor Hope Carpenter*

• DIY Projects •

Create Your Own Vision Board

I have used vision boards at work and in my life as a coach and now ladies are gathering together and having their own vision board parties. These vision boards can be about your spiritual journey, your journey through life, your children, your family or whatever you desire. The idea is to take a large poster board, glue, tape, scissors, magazines (all types of magazines), craft items, pictures (whatever you want to use). To make it extra fun have wine, cheese, bread, and nice music. Then begin to create your vision board. Give everyone 1 to 2 hours to complete their board. Upon completion, each person will get a chance to share their story and present their boards. It's a wonderful opportunity to learn more about your sisters/friends connect on a deeper level, reflect and bond. At the end, take pictures and share them with each other.

~ *Vecepia Robinson* ~

Removing Oil Stains from Clothes

To remove oil stain from the clothes you need:

- Baking soda
- Dawn soap
- Hydrogen peroxide
- Toothbrush (old)

Spray hydrogen peroxide on stain until completely soaked. Put a small amount of dawn soap, sprinkle baking soda, brush with toothbrush into a nice paste. Let it stand 30 min then wash.

~ *Martha "Matti" Medina* ~

· DIY Projects ·

How to Remove Blood Stains from Clothes

Use ammonia or white vinegar OR.. are you ready? WD-40!!! Spray on stain, let it sit, scrub with toothbrush, and launder as normal.

∼ Hope Carpenter ∼

Projects & Outings

Get a membership card at the library. On their site they usually have things and tickets for families to experience activities around the surrounding cities.

∼ Khaliah Calderon ∼

Getting Rid of Cooking Smells

How to get rid of the smell of eggs after cooking. In a bowl of water add a cup of vinegar. Wash your pans and rinse on the vinegar water.

∼ Ananda Variganji ∼

> Jesus didn't bail on your brokeness.
> *Pastor Hope Carpenter*

· DIY Projects ·

Cleaning Stainless Steel Appliances – Chemical Free!

Materials:
- spray bottle with white vinegar
- olive oil or any cooking oil
- soft cloth

Instuctions:
- Find the direction of the grain on the applianc.
- Spray vinegar on the surface and wipe with cloth in the direction of the grain.
- Dip cloth in a small amount of oil and polish appliance in direction of the grain.

~ *Shaundra Davis* ~

Wanna watch Netflix or use your phone in the shower?

Things needed:
- Phone
- Tape
- Ziplock bag

Just put your phone in the ziplock bag, put the tape on bag and stick it under your shower cap!

~ *Yasi Figueroa* ~

· DIY Projects ·

Styling/Staging

Styling (also known as staging) specific rooms or spaces in your home is a great way to keep your space feeling fresh and satisfying, and it's easier than you might imagine! Creating a vignette is one component of styling. It's essentially bringing together an intentional grouping of accessories. Strategically placed as a vignette, these items tell a story or evoke a feeling. They can be large or small, permanent or refreshed with the seasons.

Start by identifying what special space you want to style. Some ideas are: a blank wall at the end of a hallway, a blah kitchen countertop, the wall above the fireplace, or a front foyer. Choose the space you want to set up your vignette, and start the process by decluttering! Put away all that you can so that neighboring flat surfaces are clean and clear, and are no longer unnecessarily distracting to your eye. This will make a tremendous difference, as too many competing objects will only feel overwhelming! Remember, you want your vignette to be a point of focus and an enjoyable place for your eyes to rest.

Choose a theme for your vignette. What story do you want to tell here? Then choose accessories that help tell that story. Balance is key, and is accomplished by choosing accessories that are of various heights. Place the items, then step back and evaluate. Play with their placement until the vignette makes you smile! Below are some examples to get your imagination flowing.

Let's create a vignette to style a console in your livingroom. Let's use:

- Example of tall item: A large, framed photo or artwork with an impactful image hung above the console. Perhaps you could use a photo of gently flowing water in a stream.
- Example of medium item: In front of the photo on the console, place a beautiful green fern in a heavy stone pot.

· DIY Projects ·

- Example of short item: Let the eye travel up and down your vignette, making this short item your low point. Here, nestle a bowl of river rocks either closely tucked next to and in front of the fern, or opposite the fern. Go with what feels right for the placement.
- Example of (optional) trailer: A trailer helps your eye gently move away from clustered objects, kind of like how a mountain descends from a peak to a plain (think gradual descent and trailing away). Maybe use a worn branch from a tree, or real antlers. Place it opposite the fern, at the other side of the photo. Trailers work well on long surfaces, such as consoles or fireplace mantels where you want to extend the reach of your vignette but keep the main accessories snuggled together as a unit.
- Next, let's create a kitchen vignette together. Let's use:
- Example of tall item: Beautiful olive wood cutting board with a hand-carved handle. Rest it on your backsplash with the handle up to create height.
- Example of medium item: An antique butter crock (heavy stoneware open jar) with a rosemary plant tucked inside. Place to one side of the cutting board.
- Example of short item: On the opposite side of the cutting board, lay your favorite Italian cookbook down flat on the countertop (with the spine facing out). Choose a cookbook that has a beautiful cover, and ideally in a color that compliments the accent color in the room.
- Example of (optional) trailer: Place a beautiful, large tomato on the cookbook, and another just off to the side like it is trailing away from the collection of items.

≈ *Jenny Hoyt* ≈

> Your happiness
> will always be at risk
> until you detach yourself
> from earthly things.
>
> *Pastor Hope Carpenter*

organizational hacks

> "
> For which of you, desiring to build a tower, does not first sit down and count the cost.
> "
>
> Luke 14:28

· Organizational Hacks ·

Bundle Buddy – Jewelry Organizer

Organize that clump of jewelry into pretty colorful bags. No more tangles, easy access, and beautiful to look at. This saved me time in the morning, every little bit helps.

≈ *Sandra Sanchez* ≈

- -

Keeping the House Clean in 15 Minutes

As a single mom with four children at home, keeping the house clean and organized can present a formidable challenge. I've instituted a fifteen minute clean up time at the end of each day. I bring the children into the kitchen/living area of my home and set the microwave timer for fifteen minutes. We spend this time picking up and organizing our things together, which helps teach the children responsibility, while also encouraging teamwork. Many hands make light work!

≈ *Tana Romine* ≈

- -

Toys toys and more Toys - How to save money!

So many of us mothers/fathers haved loved our children so much with birthday and Christmas presents to our children. Here is a good idea to save money and help with the toy clutter. So, you get several boxes depending on what you want to store and the toys you don't see your kids play with box them up and date it. After about 3 to 6 months rotate the toys. Your children will be so exited to play with toys they haven't seen in a while and you can save money!

≈ *Carla Johnson* ≈

· Organizational Hacks ·

Traveling Tips

I travel a lot, so my tips are traveling tips. Some tips are super basic like roll your clothes; you can pack more and your clothes have less wrinkle. I can change three times a day on an 11 day trip without going over the 50 lb luggage limit. Be sure to squeeze all the air out of your shampoos, lotions, and conditioners and then put them in a Ziploc bag. Bring extra Ziploc bags. I also pack a huge empty "cute" bag for souvenirs. It also works great as your "purse" traveling on the way home because somehow my luggage is usually 65 lbs on the way home and I need to stuff my "purse" and my carry on bag with the extra poundage. I ALWAYS travel with wipes. Not only do I use them but I become everyone's hero when they need one!

At home and in my car I usually have a half packed suitcase which works for the next trip for emergencies ie. hospital stay, unexpected sleepover. I also leave shoes and flip flops in my car for a shoe emergency. It has paid off.

Packing Fashion Show

For the big trips like Italy, Israel, Spain, Dominican Republic, Cabo San Lucas, etc. I like to have a "packing" Fashion Show. I have had fashion shows for My mom (she now lives in Heaven), my aunt, my grandson, my daughter, etc ... I try on EVERY outfit that I consider taking on the trip. I mix and match my clothes, shoes, hats, and swim wear to create different looks throughout the trip. This actually eliminates bringing along too many pairs of shoes (which helps to stay under the 50 pound luggage limit). It helps so that you do not overpack or underpack. This is also helpful to see what you may need to purchase to supplement the vacation wardrobe. (Note: after the show I iron and then roll up all my clothes and place them in the suitcase! – Linen does not wrinkle as much when you roll it).

~ *Lisa Landavazo* ~

Organizing Accessories

Too many purses, hats, neck-ties, etc. Purchase door hangers, put on closet doors, bathroom doors, and or others doors. Door hangers hold 12 plus items. Place 2 different door hangers on opposite sides of the door (24 plus items.)

Organizing Time

Everyday pick one room to organize including closets, dishes, mopping, or paper work etc. You'll feel good about your progress in a short time. Remember to pray and study first. Finally, always pray before bedtime.

~ *Florence Jones* ~

Hang More Clothes In Your Closet

Use the soda ring from a can as a way to hang more clothes in your closet. Put the ring around the top of a hanger with garment and then attach another hanger with garment to ring. It maximizes space!

~ *Charlene Smith* ~

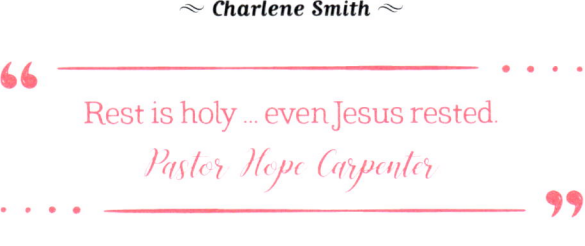

> Rest is holy ... even Jesus rested.
> *Pastor Hope Carpenter*

· Organizational Hacks ·

Keeping Nail Polish Organized

For organizing your nail polish(for those with a big collection), you can use clear glass cookie jars to store them in! Sort them out by color and shades for extra aesthetic.

∾ *Chanlin Guthrie* ∾

- -

Kitchen Counter Cleaning

In a bottle, mix water and white vinegar and a little bit of soap. This makes a great DIY cleaning supply for kitchen counters or anything around your house.

∾ *Lucy Toscano* ∾

- -

Preparing Your Dog(s) for the New Baby

Two months prior to the baby arriving, we started washing our clothes in the baby detergent we were going to use for the baby so the dogs could get familiar with the smell and associate the smell with us. The next stage was when the baby was born. Before our new baby came home, we brought home the blanket that the baby was wrapped in at the hospital to let the dogs smell it and get familiar with the smell.

∾ *Diana Rodriguez* ∾

" Rejoice when others are blessed.
Pastor Hope Carpenter "

· Organizational Hacks ·

Getting Stains Out of Food Containers

After using plastic containers for some time, the food containers get stained. To get rid of the stains, put these in the hot sun during summer and the stains will disappear.

~ *Ananda Variganji* ~

Getting the Kids & Family Ready for the Week

If you have children and work, get your children's clothes out on Saturday night for the week. Socks, underwear, tops and bottoms then place backpacks ready for the next day with shoes at the door.

~ *Carole Stanford* ~

Write It All Down Philosophy

If it isn't written it won't get done. Use notes app on your iPhone or create a spread sheet on Google Drive and download app so you could work on your list from your phone or computer. Mine is named "Moreno to do list" and has several tabs: home to do this week and to do this month, to buy, to visit my family. Also share a sheet on the drive for budget we match with our bank and keep track of our expenses as we go. I strongly recommend the Dollar app from Dave Ramsey on tips to save money and be wise with it.

~ *Stephanie Moreno* ~

· Organizational Hacks ·

5 Tips for New Mommies

1. Do not be so hard on yourself: You are doing an excellent job already, parenthood is not easy and you will learn as you go with what works best for you and your children.

2. So Important to Give Yourself "Alone Time": After all that you went through, it is so important as part of the recovery process to take some time for you to get your mind, body and soul recovered from all that just happened.

3. Try to write it all down: As a new mom and organized freak soon after having my daughter, I realized I couldn't keep the same pace and schedule I had before her. I would sometimes miss or forget the stuff I needed to complete for the day such as laundry, dishes, put something on the mail, fill out forms, or make a shopping list. So I decided to make a list on a notepad or even on my phone the night before or morning before she would wake up and I would write down all the stuff I wanted to complete. This was so helpful because it made me feel good knowing I was finishing my tasks on the side while taking care of my daughter. It made me feel proactive.

4. Update Your Wardrobe: It might take a bit to get that body back but who says you need to wear maternity clothes for the rest of the year? Go ahead and shop for new clothes that make you feel comfortable and confident. This was part of the recovery for me, it helped me remember who I was before my daughter was born.

5. Begin the sleep-in-crib training after 3 months: This is so important because the sooner your child falls into the routine of sleeping on his/her own crib, the sooner you'll get a much more sound and comfortable sleep. Even if the baby still wakes up in the middle of the night to feed. It is so much easier as the months go by, specially if you are the caregiver, you need a good sleep to be alert and recuperated for the next day.

∾ *Stephanie Moreno* ∾

> Don't treat your spouse the way they treat you... treat your spouse the way God treats you.
>
> *Pastor Hope Carpenter*

date night ideas

> "
> Don't stay in an
> unhealthy relationship
> just to be accepted
> "

Pastor Hope Carpenter

· Date Night Ideas ·

Saturday Night Fun
- Cruising Around Town
- Drive-in Theater
- Fire Pit at the Beach
- Ghost Tour
- Indie Movie Night
- Jazz Club
- Karaoke
- Line Dancing
- Local Festival
- Swing Dancing

Classic Dates
- Carnival
- Dinner and a Movie
- Stargazing
- Walk on the Beach
- Watch the Sunrise or Sunset

Daytime Dates
- Aquarium
- Art Gallery
- Bird-Watching
- Botanical Garden
- Farmers Market
- Fly a Kite
- Hayride
- House Hunting
- Museum
- Planetarium
- Picnic at the Park
- Walking Tour
- Wimdow Shopping
- Zoo

· Date Night Ideas ·

Eat, Drink & Be Married
- Brunch & Mimosas
- Cheese Tasting
- Chocolate Tasting
- Coffee Date
- Dinner Cruise
- Fondue
- Food Tasting Fair
- Happy Hour
- Ice Cream/Fro-Yo
- Mystery Dinner
- Seafood
- Wine Tasting

Fun at Home
- Board Games
- Champagne by the Fire
- TV Series Marathon
- Video Game Night

Be Entertained
- Comedy Club
- Concert
- Cover Band
- Improv
- Opera
- Orchestra
- Theatre

His Turn to Pick
- Racetrack (Horses or Cars)
- Sports Bar
- Test Drive a Sports Car
- Video Arcade

Your Turn to Pick
- Antique Shopping
- Couples Massage
- Day at the Spa

· Date Night Ideas ·

Get Sporty
- » Basketball
- » Batting Cages
- » Bike Ride
- » Bowling
- » Camping
- » Frisbee
- » Gold/Driving Range
- » Hiking
- » Ice Skating
- » Indoor Climbing Gym
- » Jet Skis
- » Kayaking
- » Kickboxing
- » Mini Golf
- » Paintball
- » Rafting
- » Scuba Diving
- » Surfing
- » Swimming
- » Tandem Biking
- » Tennis
- » Work Out

Pure Adventure
- » Amusement Park
- » Balloon Ride
- » Bed and Breakfast
- » Camping
- » Helicopter Ride
- » Horseback-Riding
- » Sailing
- » Skydiving
- » Swim with Dolphins
- » Tubing Down the River

Take a Class
- » Dance Class
- » Painting Class
- » Pottery Class

> "Every time you think good about your spouse, tell them.
> *Pastor Hope Carpenter*"

my peeps

Name _____   Name _____

Phone _____   Phone _____

Email _____   Email _____

Name _____   Name _____

Phone _____   Phone _____

Email _____   Email _____

Name _____   Name _____

Phone _____   Phone _____

Email _____   Email _____

Name _____   Name _____

Phone _____   Phone _____

Email _____   Email _____

my peeps

Name _____ Name _____
Phone _____ Phone _____
Email _____ Email _____

Name _____ Name _____
Phone _____ Phone _____
Email _____ Email _____

Name _____ Name _____
Phone _____ Phone _____
Email _____ Email _____

Name _____ Name _____
Phone _____ Phone _____
Email _____ Email _____

my peeps

Name _____   Name _____

Phone _____   Phone _____

Email _____   Email _____

Name _____   Name _____

Phone _____   Phone _____

Email _____   Email _____

Name _____   Name _____

Phone _____   Phone _____

Email _____   Email _____

Name _____   Name _____

Phone _____   Phone _____

Email _____   Email _____

my peeps

Name _____ Name _____
Phone _____ Phone _____
Email _____ Email _____

Name _____ Name _____
Phone _____ Phone _____
Email _____ Email _____

Name _____ Name _____
Phone _____ Phone _____
Email _____ Email _____

Name _____ Name _____
Phone _____ Phone _____
Email _____ Email _____

> Jesus loves you. Wants you. He doesn't just tolerate you. You belong. You have a place at His table. You are not trash. You never were. You are beloved by the King of the Universe. You have a future. Face forward. Death is behind you. Life is ahead of you.
>
> *Pastor Hope Carpenter*